Unlocking Legacies & Releasing Burdens

Dr. Gayl Crump Swaby
Unlocking Legacies & Releasing Burdens

Published by BooxAi
ISBN: 979-8-9854129-0-1

Unlocking Legacies & Releasing Burdens

How to Let Go of Generational Traumas & the Wounds that Keep Us Chained to the Past

Dr. Gayl Crump Swaby

A 5-WEEK ONLINE COURSE

A 5-WEEK ONLINE COURSE

As a thank you gift for purchasing my book, you will receive two bonus items, 100% free.

BONUS ITEMS (VALUED AT $599.00) INCLUDE:

*FREE ACCESS TO MY 5-WEEK UNLOCKING LIMITING BELIEFS ONLINE COURSE

*FIVE 15-MINUTE 1-ON-1 POWER COACHING SESSIONS
WITH A PROFESSIONAL COACH/COUNSELOR

NEWGENCONSULTS.COM/COURSE

"Break Every Chain"

This book is dedicated to
my children, Carlos Jr. and Kaelyn,

hope

If you only carry one thing throughout your entire life, let it be hope. Let it be hope that better things are always ahead. Let it be hope that you can get through even the toughest of times. Let it be hope that you are stronger than any challenge that comes your way. Let it be hope that you are exactly where you are meant to be right now, and that you are on the path to where you are meant to be... Because during these times, hope will be the very thing that carries you through.

- Nikki Banas

This book is also dedicated to my brother, Link,
who left us too soon but will always be remembered by these two
words he used at the end of every text message,
"GIVE THANKS."

Foreword

There is no better time than now for a work of knowledge, understanding, and compassion such as the book that you are about to read by my friend, Dr. Gayl Crump Swaby. The resources and information provided in these pages can open your eyes to a new world.

Anxiety, toxic stress, and pressures of life bombard each of us every single day. The world seems to be spinning faster and more out of control than ever. The individual hurts and disappointments in life must be dealt with in a calm and assuring manner. The pressures of life overwhelm adults while the youth are experiencing stress from every side that no other generation has endured before. However, there is *hope*. There is always **hope**. The very book that you have in your hands is a great place to start.

The work of Dr. Gayl Crump Swaby is tremendous, and the way she influences so many people in her community and around the world does not go unnoticed. As you read *Unlocking Legacies & Releasing Burdens*, you will discover that life is full of many different hurts, pains, and traumas, and if we are not prepared to face those storms head-on, then healing will be delayed, if not unattainable.

I have come to know Gayl and have admired her heart and her work for many years. One of her many traits that is immediately recognized is her compassion for others. She has a tremendous gift of teaching, training, and sharing her wisdom with so many others that will soon be released to the world to counsel hundreds of other hurting people. She is truly a champion for those who have been hurt, and this book is just a glimpse of her wealth of knowledge.

The importance of breaking the cycle of generational traumas is huge in this world that is continually being filled with more stress and anxiety as each day goes by. The tools and techniques found within these pages are tried and proven to help. Read this book, take notes, and underline, circle, and highlight the paragraphs that touch you. Make *Unlocking Legacies & Releasing Burdens* your **life workbook** that you will not only read once but will also keep handy to help you throughout the many years to come.

Just when you feel the storms will overtake you… Just when you feel that darkness could not get any darker... The rain begins to stop, and the clouds begin to part. Then the most miraculous gift of promise appears through the fading clouds—a rainbow. The promise of **hope**.

This book will be the beginning of that realization of **hope**.

Dr. Gregory Williams

Author of *Shattered by the Darkness: Putting the Pieces Back Together After Child Abuse* and *When Dark Clouds Come: The Road Map to HOPE*

gawilli1@texaschildrens.org

ENDORSEMENTS

Unlocking Legacies & Releasing Burdens is an important addition to the theories addressing the mental health of BIPOC (Black, Indigenous, People of Color). Dr. Gayl Crump Swaby uses her personal experiences, her academic research, her travels, and her professional training to develop a book that is insightful, engaging, informative, and transformative. She challenges people of color to recognize the historical impact of White supremacy on our mental health, our self-esteem, and our personal and collective development. Dr. Swaby examines the damage done in the United States by a history of slavery, Jim Crow, and racism. Her approach uses a variety of tools to address this legacy, including several methods developed by her (e.g., P.A.U.S.E. and the collective care wheel).

This book can be helpful to clinicians and clients who are struggling with intergenerational trauma and are looking for culturally competent methods to address the long-term psychological impact of oppression and White supremacy. *Unlocking Legacies & Releasing Burdens* is not a passive and abstract approach to this intergenerational trauma but a call to action for personal and collective healing for communities of color. This book encourages healing using a step-by-step approach to the healing process. In a time of increased White supremacy, as evidenced by attacks on Critical Race Theory and The 1619 Project, this is a much-needed volume to encourage wholeness and healing.

Edith C. Fraser, PhD, ACSW, LICSW
Retired Professor and Coauthor of *Saving Marriage by Applying Biblical Wisdom*

When I read the opening chapter from *Unlocking Legacies & Releasing Burdens,* I was immediately engaged and enthralled. The words are so powerfully crafted by Dr. Gayl Crump Swaby that they immediately spoke to me in a deeply personal and reflective way. In fact, the honesty in which Dr. Swaby shared her narrative gave me permission to interrogate and revisit my past traumatic experiences and those within my family that I still carry.

Unlocking Legacies & Releasing Burdens provides the reader, who may be bearing longstanding and generational trauma, with a pathway to freedom from wounds held much too long. In this time when biological, economic, racial, social and emotional pandemics plague people, especially those who are Black, people of color, vulnerable and marginalized, Dr. Swaby's book comes at the right time. It is healing centered and will become a balm in Gilead for anyone who reads it. I recommend it with boundless enthusiasm.

Ron Walker, Executive Director
The Coalition of Schools Educating Boys of Color

Gayl Crump Swaby has written a must-read for any person of color who wants to transform their life from generational trauma to healing. *Unlocking Legacies & Releasing Burdens* encourages the reader to go below the surface of deeply rooted culturally burdensome beliefs to release them and to take control of their path to wellness for themselves and the generations to come.

Julia Mejia, Boston City Councilor At-Large
Chair of the Committee on Civil Rights
Chair of the Committee on Small Business,
Workforce Development

Compounded on top of our legacy of communal trauma, which existed pre-COVID, we are going through a pandemic while in a time of race reckoning. Our trauma is at an all-time high. Dr. Crump Swaby has provided a life-and-academic informed guide that helps us not only as individuals but as a People.

James 'Jimmy' Hills, Host,
#javawithjimmy|Mental Health Advocate

Contents

Healing is weird.
Some days you're okay and you're doing just fine. Other days it still hurts like it's fresh. It's a process with no definitive time frame. You just have to keep going and know that when all is said and done, you're going to be okay.

Unknown Author

Introduction

"If you don't heal what hurt you, you will bleed on people who didn't cut you." ~Unknown

"By going through the agony of healing, you no longer pass the poison chalice onto the generations that follow. It is incredibly important and sacred work." ~Unknown

"No Woman, No Cry" ~ Bob Marley

Vulnerability. "No Woman, No Cry" by Bob Marley is usually the song I hum along to when I am hurt and denying myself of feelings, especially those that lead to emotions that make me want to weep. As a result, both in the past and sometimes now, I have gone through life without the ability to be my authentic self with the people I love—not because I wanted to, but because I couldn't or wouldn't allow myself to be vulnerable. I simply couldn't permit myself to feel then and still have days when I deny myself permission to feel now. However, lately, I have been spending a considerable amount of time reflecting on who I am, who I want to be, who I am becoming, and how I want to move in the world. To say it has been a challenge is an understatement; still, I am learning and growing. I am making the conscious decision to "sit with me" and to evolve.

After the passing of my father, I have learned things about myself and my history that have rocked my world. This process began eight years ago, which was two years after my father died. I remember the day I received the phone call like it was yesterday. I was on my way to a client's home for a counseling session, and my father had been in the hospital for more than a week after being rushed to the ER during his weekly dialysis treatment. It was October 16, 2010, just after 2:00 p.m., when my brother called to deliver the news. As I listened to him relay the message, I went completely numb as I continued driving.

The closer I got to my destination, the more I realized I needed to call someone. I couldn't decide whom I should call first, my husband or my supervisor. I opted for my supervisor because I needed someone to say to me, "*Stop!* Don't go any further. You need to cancel your appointment." And that's what happened. My supervisor asked where I was, and I told her I was on my way to a client's house and tried to convince her that I would be okay and would cancel all other clients after that one. She immediately talked some sense into me and told me to go home. She assured me she would call my clients and cancel my appointments—all of them. I was thankful because if she had left it up to me, I'm sure I would have kept going and would have continued to see every client on my schedule. For me, it would have been business as usual.

After speaking with my supervisor, I called my husband and informed him of my father's passing. He was very supportive and asked where I was and whether I wanted him to leave work and meet me at home. I told him no and guaranteed that I was headed home and would be fine. To this day, I cannot recall whether I cried; it is still a blur.

I drove around for what felt like hours and eventually found my way home. I later called my mother, who was still at the hospital with one of my older sisters and my youngest brother. We talked for a bit, and then I started to think about all the things I had planned for after work. I was home earlier than expected, and I needed to fill the time and the void I was feeling. I remembered I had a meeting at my children's school, and despite what or how I was feeling, which I didn't comprehend at the moment, I made the decision to attend the scheduled board meeting; I was a member, after all. Besides, I needed to think about other things. I needed to occupy my mind with anything else other than my father's death. I was that strong, stereotypical Black woman…the one Bob Marley sang about…the one who doesn't cry.

A few hours had passed since my brother's call, and I was at the meeting. Yet all I could focus on was my father and trying to understand the impact of his death on me. I was on the schedule to make a presentation to the school board, but I couldn't focus on the here and now. Questions and thoughts kept circling in my head. *What does this all mean to me? And for me?* There were no answers.

What I do remember is waking up the next morning and saying to myself, *Something has got to change.* I was not sure what, but the thought would haunt me over the next two years. It wasn't until when I found myself sitting on my therapist's couch on the anniversary of the day my father had passed with the same question lingering in my hippocampus that I had a breakthrough. Even now when I recall this moment, I have to stop telling the story several times. The tears are still fresh, as though his passing happened just yesterday. I must believe it was because I never really shed any tears then, which frees me to shed them now. I had not grieved for my father, and I am keenly aware of this now.

This story is only a preview of what led me to write *Unlocking Legacies & Releasing Burdens*. This book is about the many unspoken burdens I have carried all my life that are not mine to carry, nor should be given to others to carry. These are the legacies that hold secrets, joys, sadness, and, of course, burdens—some good, some bad, but hardships, each and every one. There's no greater journey than the one within.

I spend a lot of time standing in front of people teaching, presenting workshops, leading seminars, or speaking. When I am not doing that, I see a handful of clients in my private practice. A lot of my topics center around trauma and healing. As a professor, many of the courses I teach or have taught focus on training students to become mental health professionals by integrating cross-cultural approaches to the treatment of mental illness and other stress-related life challenges. I have been teaching for more than fifteen years, as a full-time professor for one college and as an adjunct at several others. You can imagine the number of students who have crossed my path.

In the last two years, I've been focusing my work on historical and intergenerational trauma, as well as the legacy and ancestral burdens and their impact on my own life. Because of this new focus, my workshops, seminars, or speaking engagements now concentrate on how legacy and ancestral burdens play a massive role in how people see themselves and the world around them. I talk about the history of Black people and the impact of slavery. Then I talk about how we have held on to beliefs that are not our own to hold or to carry. These beliefs are crippling our families, our communities, and our young people.

It is at this point that I think about my father's death and how he lived his life. He never stopped to smell the roses; he believed that to show emotion and to not work hard were forms of weakness. To be "human" was not encouraged and was looked upon as a deficit.

I look back at my choice not to allow myself to be present in the moment of feeling the death of my father. I think of myself and many others because these burdens we are carrying are keeping us imprisoned, shackled, chained, and enslaved emotionally, physically, spiritually, and psychologically. I have to talk about it so that others can release their burdens and create new, different legacies that will bring healing to their families, their communities, and our youth.

It was only through my time spent in therapy that I came to the following revelation. Throughout my life, I have always been committed to my cultural upbringing: the values, morals, and beliefs that were instilled in me. I never questioned my parents when they told me anything that I felt deep within me didn't make sense. I dared not challenge them or even outwardly show I disagreed or had any thoughts about anything different from what they were telling me. I was a strong proponent of respecting other people's cultural beliefs, attitudes, and values. Then a colleague of mine once said to me, "Not everything cultural makes it okay or makes it right." Those words confirmed my revelation, and it was then that I knew releasing my burdens would be necessary. With this revelation came the first part of my breakthrough, which led to the breakdown of any belief I held on to about culture and what had kept me from seeing and understanding at a deeper level.

The next revelation I had came in 2018. I attended a workshop that talked about legacy burdens. This spurred my second breakthrough as to where these beliefs and structures I had become accustomed to and depended on had infiltrated my being without me realizing it.

In 2017, I was invited to speak at a prestigious college in Massachusetts to a group of 100 freshmen women of color about self-care. I learned that every year the college accepted 100 young women of color from top high schools who were usually in the top 5 % of their graduating class. As I prepared for this talk, I inquired about the population demographics of the group. What I learned was that they were mostly first-generation college students from all over the world. I also learned that many of these girls didn't get to choose the course of study they would major in or pursue as a career. They were expected to fulfill a legacy of success that was passed down from one family member to another—with the added pressure that they had achieved more educationally than their families. Often they arrived at college with predetermined goals and expectations.

These expectations were so high and increasingly demanding that it often led to stress, depression, anxiety, anorexia, and other mental health issues. They were considered the best of the best and were expected to maintain that status at any cost. The administration and director of the program had come to realize what had been happening throughout the years and invited me to talk about the importance of self-care. On the day of my talk, the director of the program introduced me, and it was time for me to stand before those eager young women and share my tips for self-care.

As I looked out into that auditorium and into the eyes of those young women, the introduction of my speech changed. I froze, looked at the outline of my written speech, then looked back into the auditorium. What I saw was myself at 16 years old. Yes, 16—the age I graduated from high school and enrolled as a freshman at Oakwood University in Huntsville, Alabama. I had left my birthplace of St. Croix in the Virgin Islands, the place I had spent the first 16 years of my life, and was living in a new place, away from my family and my island home. I made an agreement with myself to work hard at any cost, even if I didn't feel good. My parents had sent me there for one thing and one thing only: to get an education and a degree. Nothing else mattered.

I looked out at those freshmen women and realized that I had a lot in common with them. It was time for me to unlock a belief I had been carrying and release that burden by allowing myself to be vulnerable, transparent, and present in front of these girls without trepidation. I could hear the voices of my father and mother: "Don't air your dirty laundry," "Don't tell other people your business," and "Keep it to yourself." Ringing in my ears were these four statements: "Don't talk; don't feel; don't trust. Pretend nothing is happening."

Deep down inside, standing in front of these young women, I knew I couldn't hold that belief any longer. I felt an inner turmoil. I couldn't stand still. There was an internal war happening, and I was the only one who could put a stop to it. So I did. I shared a part of my true self, a part of my story with these young women. It was the first time I had taken the leap of faith outside of my therapist's office, and though it was terrifying, *it felt good.* I had finally begun my journey to wellness.

In case you don't already know, this book is about healing—healing the pains of our past and releasing those things that have been keeping us in psychological and emotional bondage. *It's a journey.*

In this book, I talk about the many burdens we carry as Black people. Burdens are passed down from generation to generation, and many of these started or were inherited from our ancestors who were enslaved. I talk about historical and intergenerational traumas and how these experiences have continued to cause havoc in our lives and the lives of our children, our families, and our communities. I speak of the legacies that have become burdensome to a point where it causes our health to fail, our souls to weep, and our minds to be distracted.

One purpose of this book is to bring awareness to Black people about the importance of understanding where some of our beliefs about mental and physical health, and our spiritual practices might stem from. This book is for my brothers and sisters of the African diaspora. Whether you are African, African American, Afro-Caribbean, or Afro-Latinx, *Unlocking Legacies & Releasing Burdens is for you.* What it is not is an exhaustive revelation of legacy burdens due to the breadth and depth within the African diaspora. Although I understand that legacy and ancestral burdens are not limited to just Blacks, this book will unapologetically focus on those Blacks of the African diaspora.

Throughout this book, you will see many references to music and songs. I love music, and I have found that listening to certain artists and/or genres helps to feed my soul. Music reduces stress and comforts me. It lifts my spirits and energizes me when I feel down. It helps me to think more clearly when I am struggling through difficult times, and it reminds me of the beauty in the world and how much I have in common with others.

There are also messages in songs and in lyrics that help soothe the melodies that play loudly in the depths of one's mind and soul. Today, I use music to deal with my feelings, to express myself, and to connect with others. Music helps me to stay happy and to be productive. I hope that the messages I share throughout this book resonate with you, helping you to tap into your inner workings and leading you toward a profound sense of self-awareness and healing.

"A PEOPLE MUST KNOW THEIR ORIGINS AND PRACTICE THEIR TRADITIONS IN ORDER TO BE THEMSELVES. IF NOT, THEY LOSE THEMSELVES IN ANOTHER'S VISION OF REALITY. AND IF THAT REALITY IS THE CREATION OF THEIR ENEMY, THEN THEY FALL DEEPLY ASLEEP IN SOMEONE ELSE'S NIGHTMARE."

MWALIMU K. BOMANI BARUTI

CHAPTER 1

THE BEGINNING

HISTORICAL AND INTERGENERATIONAL TRAUMA

"People are trapped in history, and history is trapped in them."

~James Baldwin

Trauma has been a buzzword for the past several years, in social media, mass-market articles, and television series, to name a few examples. Along with the layperson interest, counseling professionals have been working on many different models of treatment focused on helping those living with past or current traumas to heal.

There has also been a greater emphasis on the traumatic experiences faced by many Blacks. Trauma-informed care and practices have been at the center of discussions when it comes to working with marginalized communities and primary communities of color. These practices have been used to assist those who are not "trauma specialists," yet have a method by which they engage or intervene when working with individuals and families.

Before we can begin the discussion about what legacy burdens are, we must first start the conversation as to their origin. One cannot understand legacy burdens without understanding history's impact on these burdens.

First, I will provide you with several working definitions of trauma and its relation to these legacy burdens. I will make a distinction between historical trauma and intergenerational trauma.

Trauma Defined

Here are a few working definitions.

- It is caused by an event that overwhelms a person's mental ability to cope.
- It can stem from a wide array of natural or human-made events. [The impact of the event can create a mental and neurological representation and/or have a physical manifestation. These manifestations can be independent of the actual trauma event. (Mohatt 2014)]

Trauma Explained

Symptoms of the impact may emerge over time.

Trauma victims can become reenactors but may be unconscious. The presentation can be relational or communal. With victim and perpetrator, trauma becomes relational; with victim, perpetrator, and bystanders, trauma becomes communal. Traumatic reenactment can be thought of as "living in the unremembered past." (Bloom 1996)

Historical Trauma Defined

It can be defined as the remembered mental representation of a wounding event. The event becomes historical because it is shared across the passage of time. It is complex in that it is collective.

It is experienced across generations by a group of people who share an identity, affiliation, or circumstance beyond a single familial line.

It is experienced by contemporary members not present during the past traumatizing events who may also experience trauma-related symptoms that are connected to the past event—in this case, slavery.

Intergenerational Trauma Defined

This refers to multiple familial generations but does not necessarily imply an affinity group trauma. (Straussner 2014)

Traumatic reenactment creates a "relationship between past and present, between history and our present reality, [that] has been long recognized and commented upon." (Bloom 1996)

Trauma has always been a word we associate with rape, war, abuse, natural disasters, etc., but the reality is there are many other experiences that can also be traumatic and can disrupt our lives.

At some point, we all may experience some form of trauma. It can be the death of a loved one, dealing with a serious illness, the breakup of a significant relationship, or the loss of a job.

Trauma isn't something that has to be one specific event either. "There's much more appreciation these days for micro-traumas—like chronic, more mildly traumatic things—that cumulatively, over many years, can amount to the same as one macro trauma." (Vora 2019) This is what we call big T and little T traumas.

Historical View

African Americans originate from slaves brought to the United States between 1619 and 1860. According to the US Census Bureau, 54.3% of the Black population live in the South, 18.3% in the Northeast, 18.2% in the Midwest, and 9.1% in the West. They are highly concentrated in metropolitan areas, with more than 3.7 million in the New York Metropolitan Area, 2.1 million in Atlanta, 1.7 million in Washington D.C., and 1.6 million in Chicago.

The international slave trade started with the Ndongo people, a generation of people born in Africa. In 1619, a Portuguese slave ship, the São João Bautista, traveled across the Atlantic Ocean with a casing filled with human cargo of men, women, and children. Those who were being held captive were Africans from Angola. These individuals were most likely from the kingdoms of Ndongo and Kongo, bound for a life of enslavement in Mexico. Nearly half of them died by the time the ship was seized by two English pirate ships. Those who survived the journey were taken to Point Comfort, a port near Jamestown, the capital of the English colony of Virginia. These Africans were bought and most likely worked in the tobacco fields established in the area. (Elliot 2019)

When they arrived, they were stripped of their birthright and enslaved. One way they were stripped of their birthright was with the changing of their names. This was the first essential human atrocity. The gift of the name. This was a first step in pushing them to be looked at as property or commodity. We exercise a lot of power over someone when we take their name from them. Case in point, all my life I thought my father's first name was "Jeff," until it was time for me to go to college. I needed his information to apply for financial aid and was shocked when I found out his given name was not "Jeff" but Theophilus.

The story is that my father worked for a White man when he emigrated from his birthplace of Antigua, an island in the British West Indies, to St. Croix, V.I. Because his boss thought his name was too long to pronounce, he changed it to Jeff, which became the name everyone knew my father by. When my mother first told me this story, it had no significance. However, after I started doing a lot of work around race and racism, I realized this incident was my father's experience of being stripped of his birthright.

Slaves also had their culture and traditions taken from them. You see, the slave traders didn't care about religion, culture, or traditions. They were more concerned about the political and economic goals they had to accomplish to settle the territories.

Africans and Europeans had been trading goods and people across the Mediterranean for centuries. Thus, forced labor was not uncommon. The system of slavery introduced in the early 15th century was commercialized, racialized, and inherited. Those who were enslaved were objectified and dehumanized, viewed as commodities to be exploited, bought, and sold. The sale and enslavement of the Africans on the Portuguese slave ship initiated what would later become slavery in the United States (Elliot 2019).

Slaves would soon discover sugar plantations were the most dangerous places to work. They were more dangerous in that they required the enslaved people to work long days all year. The sugar plantations served as both farm and factory. Having the Mandingo people, slaves imported from an area off the coast of Africa known as Senegambia, was important. The men were valued for their tall, athletically built, and physically fit bodies. They performed the deadliest kind of farming on the plantation. According to multiple sources, historical and modern, the primary cause of death on a sugar plantation *literally* was being "worked to death."

Then there were slaves who were captured because they were already skilled in dealing with livestock, primarily African and Native Americans. They were considered the first cowboys, captured mostly for their skills in wrangling animals.

Domestic Slave Trade

The Gold Coast area of the Deep South was where most millionaires were living in what is now the state of Louisiana, acquired by Thomas Jefferson from Napoleon Bonaparte in 1803, in a deal that doubled the size of the country and expanded the nation's slave economy. Soon after the Louisiana Purchase, which included land extending to the west and north, the United States abolished international slave trade, and thus there became a labor shortage. The slave labor rates varied across the country, and this is where they started feeling the labor shortage. At that time, the mortality rate for enslaved people was 13%; for every 100 people born, thirteen died.

However, in the Upper South (Virginia, Maryland, and the Carolinas), farming consisted of tobacco and cotton, which were nowhere near as deadly as the sugar plantations. The mortality rate for the enslaved people was averaging about 23% to 28%, and thus, despite the brutal loss of slaves that shortened their own lives, more slaves survived there than in the Deep South on sugar plantations. They had a labor surplus, and Thomas Jefferson started shipping an estimated one million enslaved people (the surplus of labor) downriver to the Gold Coast and the rest of the Deep South. This is where the term "being sent down the river" originates. No one wanted to go there. They had heard about the death rate.

The average life expectancy for someone going to work on the sugar plantation was 10 years from the day they stepped foot on the plantation, regardless of age. Enslaved people were put to work at 10 years old, both male and female. If you got there at age 10, you were most likely to die by the age of 20; if you got there at the age of 20, you were most likely to die by the age of 30, and so on.

Slaves from both the Deep South and the Upper South were auctioned off and appraised just like property. This was called chattel slavery. For example, a 25-year-old female who would normally sell for about $670 was sold for $105 because she was listed as an idiot, which depreciated her value. Another slave, a 30-year-old, and her five children, ages eight and younger, were listed as a package deal for $2,650.

The rules of enslavement in Louisiana and other French colonies were codified in Le Code Noir (Black code). Le Code Noir was authored by the Catholic church to govern slavery in any new French territory. Therefore, New France states that enslaved people never have paternal lineage records whatsoever, and maternal lineage is not attached until the age of ten. Before age 10, a person was considered a child. This meant that if a mother was sold, her children under the age of ten were sold with her as a package deal. Once children reached the age of 10, they too were considered adults.

As colonizers continued to enslave and trade, they realized they were being outnumbered by the slaves nationwide. They needed a way to keep slaves in line other than physical violence, so they used emotional, mental, and psychological tactics with a combination of violence. This is where colorism came into play. They began to give better jobs to the lighter-skinned enslaved people. They got skilled jobs and jobs in the house, and they were incentivized. This created a disconnect between the house and the field that disrupted unity and stemmed the possibility of revolt. They kept the slaves docile. The goal was to divide and conquer. The slave owners knew that a united slave rebellion would be dangerous and perhaps lead to their defeat. Thus, they used tactics to pit groups of slaves against each other.

There was a conscious and intentional attack on the family structure and education. A father might have one owner, and a mother and children have another. Children were considered property and could be sold, separating them from their mothers. Enslaved women were regularly raped and had no recourse, and laws prevented slaves from learning to read. This was by design. If just one slave became educated, then production in the field would go way down. Now all that slave would want to do is talk about what they had read. They might also, most assuredly, gain insightful and useful information to fight for their freedom. So slaves were kept from learning how to read and write. They were denied the basics of all understanding, the foundation of education, the fundamentals of reading and writing…and were expected to stay in the fields and work from sunrise to sundown for no money. The second they would have started to read and write, they would have started to imagine a different life. Managing weak and complacent slaves was a much easier way to maintain order. Slave owners controlled the flow of information to slaves because they believed it would be harder for illiterate people to succeed. Attacking the family structure, denying education, and controlling information are essential to the survival of the system.

Enslavement was used to strip slaves of their native culture, traditions, and rituals. They were prevented from even talking about them. Voodoo, for example, was a spiritual practice that was not a religion but a form of holistic medical care. However, the Catholic church demanded that all slaves be baptized. Casting Voodoo as a religion made it out to be something to be feared, and thus needed to be stamped out.

Enslaved Africans next came from the Senegambia region—Senegal and Gambia. The goal was to get the land settled and developed. It was the Catholic church that sanctioned this form of slavery. In 1452, Pope Nicholas V issued a paper bill stating that anyone who was not

Catholic or who could be considered a savage could legally be put into perpetual slavery by a Catholic person. Slavery and indentured servitude were very similar, but at least indentured servants got something in return for their service. However, slavery was different because the Pope said it was perpetual. This meant that if a mother was a slave, her child would also be a slave.

Slaves were baptized members of the Catholic church, but they were members without benefits. They were denied their last names upon their baptism and were allowed neither to pray nor to worship. They couldn't legally read (which also included reading the Bible), and if any slave was found in possession of a pencil or paper, they would receive twenty-five lashes with a bull whip; it didn't matter if they could read and write. The worst crime was slaves being caught trying to educate themselves.

Slaves usually did not even get a proper burial. They were buried in a mass grave on the plantation close to the slave quarters. If they died while working in the field, they would be tossed aside, and others would keep right on working. No one could afford to stop and carry a body all the way back to the mass grave. That kind of cruel treatment made Blacks fear and hate the Catholic church. When they were finally emancipated in 1865, they fled it in droves.

Catholicism was forced on slaves their entire life, with no kind of benefit or reward. History later showed just how extensive mass participation was in the slave trade. The Church overruled most governments. If the Pope said it, the government was most likely doing it. It was all about greed and economics. African kings and queens were trading their own people for guns and other commodities. Sadly, politics, greed, and economics were the forces behind slavery.

Centuries after slavery began, sharecropping arose as a method for freedmen to make a living shortly after their emancipation. Share-croppers would rent small plots of land on a plantation for a fixed price and turn over the sum—as a portion of their crops—to the plantation owners. But rather than earning a subsistence wage, they would often end up in debt. The first sharecropping was done for indigo—the flower used to make blue dye. Anything colored blue or purple was extremely expensive. These very rare colors were associated with royalty. That's how we got the term royal blue.

Africans who were already skilled and groomed in processing indigo were brought in to work the land and ship the goods back to France, making the slave owners rich. However, they ran into two problems. First, insect infestation destroyed almost all the crops. Then indigo started to lose profitability because it was a natural product competing against artificial colors like red dyes coming out of India.

The plantation owners started looking for a new cash crop, but they could not find it for some time, as cotton could not be grown in some areas due to the climate being far too humid. In 1795, they started growing sugar on the plantations and hit the jackpot. Everything sugar needed was right there in the Deep South: high heat and humidity. Sugar plantations had been around for years in the Caribbean, and many slaves were already groomed to work on them. There was a lot of precipitation and ample well-draining farmland. The Gold Coast had the second-longest growing season for sugar in the world, trailing the Caribbean and South America, where slavery began.

For 260 days a year, slaves would plant and tend the fields. The first weekday of January was considered the start of grinding season. The harvest started in mid-October and lasted until the week of Christmas. Slaves had Christmas and New Year's off from the fields, but then they were right back out there the rest of the season working for the next crop of cane. This schedule did not change even after emancipation, because the former slaves had limited rights. Even today, we see these same kinds of holiday/time-off structures in many organizations in communities of color, especially within school systems.

Cane farming was just like having a brand-new garden. The first month or two, a person would be out there every day, knocking out weeds and grass. Imagine people walking 1,800 acres of sugarcane rows, trimming and weeding by hand for six months. The growing season work schedule was six to seven days a week, sixteen to eighteen hours a day. If you asked slaves how long they worked, they'd tell you they worked from "can't to can't," meaning can't see to can't see.

When the grinding season started, the schedule increased to consistent seven-day work weeks—two overlapping shifts of sixteen to eighteen hours each. All slaves on the plantation worked around the clock for the entire grinding season. That's because when sugarcane is cut, it starts to rot very quickly. So it had to be cut, taken to the mill, processed, and granulated before it went bad.

When ready for harvest, sugarcane stands seven to ten feet tall. It grows so thick that it looks like one solid green wall. I remember as a young girl, growing up on the islands, watching my father plant sugarcane. He used up half of our backyard and the side of the house to plant cane, and when it grew, it was very tall. There were times at night when I would hear the bustling in the garden from my bedroom window. It was usually because it was time to harvest, and people would come at night to steal the cane before it was cut. They stole what they could and left the rest.

Cotton was King, and sugar was Queen. Queen Sugar was highly profitable, but if you weren't careful, she'd eat you right up. That's how deadly the farming was.

The sugar mills were no safer than the fields. The first step in the mill was the grinder, powered by mules. The enslaved had to work under inhumane conditions; heat strokes and heat exhaustion were common in the mill. Fatal burns, death, and infections caused by the burns were just as common.

Slavery was about economics, but it was also about racism. Africans were enslaved due to their high resistance to malaria. They were suited for the climate. If slave owners had found it economically unfeasible to enslave the Africans, they would have left them where they found them and moved right along until they found some other group better suited to handle their greedy exploits.

Ironically, African Americans who lived after slavery did more than any other generation. The first generation right out of slavery who lived from 1865 to 1920 did a lot in *and for* this country. At the time the Civil War ended, only 5% of Blacks were literate. By 1880, that number had climbed to 30%, and by 1920 it was up to 77%. Note that these numbers were self-reported, collected and published by the Census Bureau.

Newly freed Blacks embraced education, viewing it as a path to success. Shortly before the end of the Civil War, Congress established the Freedmen's Bureau to help the former slaves by providing necessities and education. Although it was initially set up to give aid to freed slaves, the Bureau also gave provisions to destitute Southern Whites. According to a paper by Robert A. Margo of the National Bureau of Economic Research, "Around 1890 the public schools of the southern states could be charitably described as backward." (Margo 1994) School administration was fragmented with many White people more interested in having children help with agriculture. Whites in charge of schools resisted the Freedmen's Bureau's efforts to educate African Americans, refusing to rent or sell schools for that purpose. The Bureau worked with African Americans to get around the resistance. Some schools were held in churches built by African Americans on land they owned; others, in makeshift shacks. The schools were staffed by volunteer teachers, both Black and White, from the North. Any African Americans in the South who could read and write helped.

Funding for Southern schools came from the state school fund, county poll taxes (which disproportionately affected African Americans, meaning that they were subsidizing White schools), and any property tax for each school district. Local school boards decided how much money each school would receive. The efforts of the Freedmen's Bureau (which ended in 1870) and African Americans' enthusiasm for learning motivated Southern Whites to take control over administration for education. The schools were segregated, and distribution of funds continued to be managed by the director of the local school board, with varying degrees of equality among states. (Margo, 1990)

The White male created social divisions founded on race, and they benefited most through huge profits from slavery and unfair practices and policies, exploiting Africans, Asians, Indians, Native Americans, and other races. They declared superiority and division of races as a means to justify inhuman activities for their personal benefit.

America's economy flourished largely thanks mostly to the labor of the enslaved Africans. Sadly, lawmakers and government officials were eager to find data that would justify forcing humans to work for no wages in terrible conditions. They also sought justification for seizing land by force from Native Americans, Mexicans, Cubans, Filipinos, Puerto Ricans, and Guamanians. They found the justification for these inequalities through faulty science, claiming groups of people with darker skin were inferior to people with White skin.

The oppressors were White Americans, who legitimized the dehumanization of entire groups of people due to skin color and differences in culture. Because these groups of people were considered intrinsically inferior, political propaganda and entrenched cultural biases created the belief that people of other races did not possess the capacity to do or be anything compared to White Americans. In other words, other people were not worthy of the same dignity and respect given to White Americans.

When America began its efforts to conquer Guam, Puerto Rico, Cuba, and the Philippines in 1898, the scientific justification of White superiority was used to rally for colonialism. Many Americans took on the notion of "The White Man's Burden," the title of a poem by Rudyard Kipling about the Philippine–American war, to bring along the inhabitants of these countries because they believed it could help advance their civilizations under American rule. Other Americans were against this imperialist idea because they thought the "White man's burden" was too heavy for another race to undertake.

This notion of inferiority has been engraved in most people's minds and must be dismantled due to its mental and psychological negative effect on the Black populace. The work ahead is great because the psychological effect is still alive and active today amid communities, families, and mindsets. The mind frame we have about slavery, inferiority, and inhumanity takes on different forms today, and its impact manifests in the fabric of generational legacies.

By 2020, it would seem as though these ignorant belief systems would have dissipated, but it is far from the reality we see and live. Slave owners used their economic powers to incorporate the working poor into their dominant structure, so that underprivileged Whites would not align with Black slaves to rise against the upper classes. This has been a political strategy that continues into modern times.

White Americans still live with the privileges they claimed upon the founding of America. Today, African Americans are still suffering from the injustices forced upon their ancestors. Despite the abolishment of slavery, the belief systems, norms, and values of White Americans at that time have not entirely disappeared. African Americans are still viewed as an inferior race by some, even though enslavement is no longer legal.

Sometimes you don't feel the weight of something you've been carrying until you feel the weight of its release.

~Unknown~

CHAPTER 2

THE LEGACY AND THE BURDEN

"No legacy is so rich as honesty."
~William Shakespeare

"Don't carry burdens that God never meant for you to carry."
~ Everlean Rutherford

"Legacy is the responsibility of the living!"
~Qwana M. "BabyGirl" Reynolds-Frasier

We all want to be remembered in a way that is positive and enlightening. Knowing the ways we lived mattered, especially to our loved ones and close friends, is important. Personally, I want to put a stamp on the future by contributing to my children and future generations. I want the mark I make to be of value and to be significant enough to encourage others to do the same as I have done or even better. For me, it's not just about money, which is a matter of importance beyond the conscious level for a Black person aware of the transatlantic slave trade, when lives like mine were sold as chattel and our labor was not valued with pay.

I care about positively affecting lives, being a good role model, making contributions, passing on lessons, and knowing I have made an impact not only on my family but also on my community—the community in which I live, my church community, and the communities I serve as an educator and therapist, locally, across the United States, and globally. Most importantly, I want to leave a legacy of promoting good health and wellness. I also want to leave money to support my children and loved ones, but what good is financial wealth if none of the other issues mentioned above have been dealt with or worked on? Financial wealth I pass down will come with other things as well—like moral responsibilities and mental wellness. I might have repressed those things to build wealth, but *at what cost*? (My therapist's favorite line) That is a legacy burden I have carried as the daughter of a family who wanted to give me wealth for security and encouraged me to get an education so that I could become financial stable for myself and future generations.

I will discuss the importance of wealth for Black people in a future chapter, primarily how it has been restricted from us, first by our being viewed as commodities without the right to own goods and later through "redlining" practices that restricted where we lived, and thus prevented access to top educational resources to advance future generations. For now, I will focus on smaller scale legacies.

Many families have legacies they pass down from one generation to the next. Some of these they are proud of…such as strength of character; loyalty to family, friends, and community; perseverance in reaching a goal; etc. These legacies can define us. Often, though, they come with unspoken expectations that get transmitted through observation and personal interactions. These well-intentioned gifts can also be a burden—pressure to succeed without emotional support, without knowing that asking for help is possible—as with the young college students of color I addressed who reminded me of who I was when I was sixteen and unaware that these things can also break us.

Then there are educational and wealth inheritance legacies, which can be both spoken and unspoken. Both may reflect positive attitudes, values, and beliefs that can make us successful in the long run, yet at times are stressful to fulfill. Let's break this down a bit. Here's an example: a father or mother attends the same prestigious college their parents attended, and so on. A parent's expectation may be that their children will attend the same school and possibly major in the same field of study, and their grandchildren will follow in their footsteps as well. But what if their children don't get into that college? What if they don't want to study the same field or pursue the same career?

The word *legacy* comes from the Latin word *"legare."* Webster's Dictionary defines it as "something transmitted by or received from an ancestor or predecessor or from the past." What I am describing are thoughts, beliefs, and values we *don't* usually define as legacies. I know that one does not necessarily have to have a traumatic experience to have a legacy burden. However, I'll be discussing legacy burdens stemming from historical trauma, and specifically in relation to Blacks within the United States. In historical terms, a legacy is something that is handed down from one period to another. Often it means something handed down from an ancestor or predecessor. Metaphorically, leaving a legacy is planting seeds in a garden you never get to see.

A family legacy is the accomplishments, beliefs, actions, and guidance you demonstrate that carry forward to future generations that allow those family members to adopt and adapt them to make their lives meaningful and fruitful, although not without complication. I was a strong proponent of respecting other people's cultural beliefs, including my parents', even when deep inside, they didn't make sense to me. In my work on trauma and healing over the last few years—both personal and professional, and always guided by therapeutic guidelines—I've been learning to let go of my legacy burdens and to help others release theirs.

Another way to look at a legacy is to view its generational transmission. Psychological and emotional inheritance can be imparted via a thought or a belief that is culturally and/or emotionally handed down from our families. These beliefs or perceptions are conveyed through words, attitudes, and actions. Whether consciously or not, we accept this inheritance and believe the substance of the legacy to be true, even if it isn't.

The intergenerational perspective is the belief that what happened in one generation will influence what happens in the older and the younger generations, even if it manifests differently. Behavior patterns, symptoms, roles, and values adopted about family members, family sources of vulnerability (as well as resilience and strength), and job choices can be transmitted from generation to generation, which then becomes the family legacy. The family then becomes the carrier of the values, myths, fantasies, and beliefs, whether conscious or unconscious, that may or may not be shared by the larger community or culture. However, this also can be considered what I call *community legacies* transmitted by a group of people who have the same beliefs, values, myths, and attitudes about the environment in which they share.

In his 1998 article titled Black Psychological Functioning and the Legacy of Slavery Myths and Realities, William E. Cross, Jr. writes:

"...the collective or group trauma model requires that we first identify a group that has experienced a jolting, unpredictable, and monstrous assault. Second, we must be able to identify an unambiguous period that marks the termination of the trauma. Then, and only then, can we establish a before-and-after frame of reference. More specifically, the experiences of the group following the trauma must be more normative or nontraumatic in nature. When these conditions are met, we document the trauma and its termination and then try to determine whether attitudes and behaviors originally elicited by the trauma have been passed down to the immediate and extended kin of the original victims, even though the survivors and their progeny live under conditions that are a far cry from the period of trauma. When such transcendence is confirmed across several decades or longer, we speak of the intergenerational legacy of the trauma."

Cross states that the trauma–transcendence–legacy model, described above, is difficult to use in thinking about African American slavery, not least of all because it was not a start-and-stop event but rather an institution lasting hundreds of years. Below I give a timeline of the impact of slavery on African Americans.

The Black Holocaust: 246 Years of Slavery 1619–1865

The enslaved were bought, bred, and sold as commodities, or like cattle, and treated as personal property. The typical slave family was matriarchal, with the mother's role being far more important than the father's to the master. Patriarchy justified slavery as the "master" being the "better man." This system of Black slavery encouraged Whites to unify around race rather than by class.

The 99 Years of Jim Crow Laws 1865–1964

In 1865, slavery (Thirteenth Amendment) and involuntary servitude were abolished, except as a punishment for crime. However, the abolishment of slavery did not make Black Americans equal under the law. They were segregated from Whites and prevented from using the same public facilities (e.g., schools, parks, libraries, even drinking fountains). In 1896, in the landmark case Plessy v. Ferguson, the US Supreme Court ruled that racial segregation did not violate the Constitution because Blacks' facilities were "separate but equal" though they were, in fact, subpar when they existed at all.

Over 100 Years of Lynching

Lynching involved the desecration of bodies, including castration. Many lynchings happened between 1882 and 1964, with at least 4,742 in Southern states and 219 in Northern. One high-profile case of lynching was the brutal murder of 14-year-old Emmett Till in 1955, which motivated young Black people to join the Civil Rights Movement.

14 Years of Fighting for Civil Rights 1954–1968

These were turbulent years of activism *and change*. In 1954, a Virginia chapter of the National Association for the Advancement of Colored People (NAACP) brought five cases challenging the racially segregated school system to the US Supreme Court *and won*. Known as Brown v. Board of Education, the lawsuits were initially led by high school students and their parents, after years of protests. Further actions occurred over these years: the Montgomery Bus Boycott, sit-ins, the March on Washington where Dr. Martin Luther King, Jr. gave his "I Have a Dream" speech, the passage of the Civil Rights Act in 1964, and, unfortunately, the assassination of Dr. King in 1968, followed by the passage of the Fair Housing Act that same year.

These events demonstrate both the effects of intergenerational legacy burden and the work to unlock the chains.

400+ Years of Oppression and Inequality 1619–2019

The many forms of oppression and inequalities that existed years ago are still present in our society today, with biases based on class, race, religion, ethnicity, immigration status, sexual orientation, and gender. Therefore, the intersection, layer, and reinforcement of ecology deprive us of a free society.

The above signifies the legacy of trauma that many Blacks have experienced. There are those who might be offended by my using the word "Holocaust," as it has always been associated with the persecution of the Jews. My question is, "Why is it okay to use the term for one group and not another?" I still believe that we should call what happened to Blacks in this country and the Caribbean what it really was—*slavery*. But the term "Black Holocaust" describes the genocide that took place. Our people were enslaved for 246 years, and institutionalized racism continues today in one form or another. This is part of our history, and though it is riddled with pain, secrecy, and shame, it is not our pain, our secret, or our shame to carry. But we carry it, nonetheless. The expression of these legacy burdens can be traced to the impact of the historical trauma of slavery experienced by many Blacks in the United States and the Caribbean.

There is a legacy of structural and institutional racism. There is also the legacy of slavery, which was a traumatic experience for our ancestors. This concept of the trauma of slavery being passed down from one generation to the next is not an easy concept to grasp. Slavery itself is a hard topic to write about. Many would argue that it is not true that the trauma of slavery has been passed down from generation to generation. How can anyone experience the aftereffects of a tragedy they have not personally experienced?

What we have are two kinds of legacies working side by side. The legacy of the Blacks, who were traumatized while being enslaved, and the legacy of the Whites, who were responsible for enslaving the Blacks—directly as slave owners or through living in a culture that perpetuates this inequality. Laws in the 1600s and 1700s divided Black slaves and White indentured servants to prevent them from joining forces against wealthy landowners. The concept of race as a form of inequality is an inheritance that Americans carry. We have both sides of the coin with contrasting views and experiences. One is purely based on economics, and the other is based on goods.

Today, many Blacks are still being enslaved by a culture of White supremacy, specifically as defined by Kenneth Jones and Tema Okun in their work "Dismantling Racism: A Workbook for Social Change Groups." They identify certain characteristics as embedded in a culture that are harmful to both Blacks and Whites. According to the website https://www.uuare.org/cwsc/, White supremacy embraces traits such as perfectionism, defensiveness, quantity over quality, individualism, and power and information hoarding. Many of these are rooted in racist beliefs, which then get placed on many Blacks just because of the color of their skin. Let's talk about them and how each one manifests, from a White supremacist perspective.

Perfectionism

Perfectionism exists as a method of power and control. It forces the person to always be vigilant and anxious. With perfectionism, there is little to no appreciation for the work people do. No opportunity is given to identify lessons learned that could be useful for improvement. There is the need to point out either how the person or work is inadequate and then to talk to others about the inadequacies of a person or their work without ever talking directly to them. The belief is that if the person makes a mistake, they are the mistake rather than it just being a "mistake." It is a condemning mindset where the focus is on targeting and devaluing an individual—rather than pointing out and rectifying an action from a stance of encouragement and improvement. The person who exerts or pushes perfectionism tends to identify what is wrong rather than what is right. All of this can lead to stress, depression, anxiety, and other mental health issues. Over time, this approach can be damaging to one's sense of self, negatively impacting self-esteem.

Defensiveness

In this situation, an organization is set up to prevent abuse and to protect the power structure that is in place. There is no interest in getting the best out of each person. It's more about who has power and how they are expected to use it. People in power who have this trait are threatened by any inkling of criticism and are viewed as inappropriate or rude. Through their defensiveness, these people create the oppressive culture.

Quantity Over Quality

The focus is on producing measurable goals. People are concerned about numbers rather than relationships; if something cannot be measured, it has no value. There's discomfort in the showing and sharing of emotions and feelings. This concept of quantity over quality comes with a price. However, it's a price slave owners are willing to pay if it enhances the content of their agenda over the people's need to be heard or engaged.

Individualism

Competition is valued, and cooperation is devalued. The ideology of individualism focuses primarily on the moral worth of the individual. The culture of individualism stresses the needs of the individual over those of the collective group. This concept views individualism as a strength. If a person is strong, self-reliant, assertive, and independent, they are considered "good." This does not align well with the belief in collectivism or cultures where characteristics such as being generous, dependable, helpful to others, and self-sacrificing are valued. So instead of evaluating people based on their ability to delegate to others and on their ability to work as part of a team to accomplish shared goals, the focus is on personal identity and autonomy.

Power and Information Hoarding

Power hoarding is just what it implies—holding on to all the power with no intention of sharing. It's the withholding of power aimed at maintaining control over those who are viewed as powerless. This can also include the withholding of information. What we find is that people who hoard power are the ones who take credit for other people's positive work performance or ideas. They pass off other people's work or ideas as their own, knowing good and well they had nothing to do with the success of the work.

At the root of power hoarding is the need for validation due to unconscious insecurities and an inferiority complex. These individuals give assignments and tasks that are impossible to carry out and limit access to only those in power. By deliberately depriving people of needed information, they increase the power of those with the information and diminish the power of those who need the information to succeed. "The only thing that white people have that Black people need, or should want, is power, and no one holds power forever," stated James Baldwin.

As we continue the discussion of legacies, we can attest to the fact that we all—in some way—adhere to or create our own histories. The histories we create are considered our personal legacy. We hold these inheritances for ourselves and do not usually share or pass them on to anyone else. But many of these personal legacies stem from family legacies. We each have individual responsibilities, and along with those come the burdens we carry that we could use some help with and support from others.

Burdens

"Burdens Are Lifted at Calvary" is a song sung in many churches. It's a song I have heard sung throughout my years attending church. This song can be associated with the scripture from the Bible that says, *"Come to me, all you who are weary and burdened, and I will give you rest."* (Matthew 11:28, NIV)

The word *burden* can have two meanings. It can mean to *carry* a heavy load of some kind or to *face* a challenging situation or trial. There is a difference between carrying something and facing something. When the scripture advises "all who are weary and burdened" to walk toward Jesus, it is prompting us to seek *freedom*. When you let go of carrying a heavy load, your hands become free. When you are no longer facing something challenging, it means that you have *overcome*; thus, it has passed.

In Matthew 11:28, the verse is a call toward freedom and victory, and, most importantly, *rest*. We cannot *rest* our mind, body, spirit, or soul unless we are *free*. Freedom is the key to overall well-being. Where there is a lack of freedom, there is bondage and imprisonment. We live imprisoned by the flawed and oppressive generational limiting beliefs that keep us in a state of imprisonment and devastating emotional cycles passed down from generations. We are carrying ancestral burdens that are no longer ours to carry. A release needs to happen so that we can live in freedom and flip the script for future generations. Instead of passing down burdens, we must pass down and plant wisdom seeds that will yield mental, emotional, and physical health and blessings in every area of life.

Think about how long it
took you to create the
patterns that have kept
you in fear and survival.
Be equally
patient with the
work to change your future.
-maryam hasnaa

CHAPTER 3

———————

TYPES OF LEGACY/ANCESTRAL BURDENS

"Are we being good ancestors?"
~Jonas Salk

"Leave your family with a legacy, not a burden."
~Chris Hogan

"What we carry defines who we are, and the effort we make is our legacy." ~Mitch Albom, Finding Chika: A Little Girl, an Earthquake, and the Making of a Family

"When thinking about life, remember this: No amount of guilt can solve the past, and no amount of anxiety can change the future."
~Anonymous

Racism has primarily been defined in terms of physical appearance, but it is not the only form of bias. During the years of legal slavery in the United States, African captives of lighter skin color were given indoor house chores deemed easier than fieldwork, setting them apart from their peers. This was one form of establishing the notion of "race" by those in power. It was a way of preventing group resistance by the enslaved and lower-class servants against plantation owners.

Historically, many atrocities have caused a lot of psychological damage that still shows up in our homes today via health, mental state, and overall behaviors. People of lower economic status continue to be exploited to this day. Additionally, given that all the systems here in America have been strategically designed for the dominant culture and society to thrive, everyone else is impacted by it as well.

American activist Tim Wise, who is White, has stated that no one raised in America can claim to be free of racist indoctrination. Those who believe that America is free of racism are only further perpetuating the crime. It is not a fact that we can negate or ignore. Instead, we must recognize racism and confront its legacy to move toward changes.

Many families choose to talk about their legacies, while others choose to hide them. Talking about legacies can be painful and also oppressive. When I think about some of the history I have inherited, I sometimes experience the memories as ghost stories or scary movies. They then get interpreted into beliefs, thoughts, or behaviors that become personal loads I carry and act out in my own behaviors or relationships.

Legacy or ancestral burdens are wounds or understandings that are inherited from our parents and/or caregivers that they themselves absorbed through generations even further back. These are feelings, beliefs, energy, and behaviors whose origins hail from the lives of ancestors. Legacy burdens are developed in two ways. They occur as embedded cultural dynamics across time (Mohatt 2014)—first, overtly when interacting with caregivers, and second, covertly by contagion in family and culture. These burdens originate from a feeling state (i.e., fear, anxiety) that is expressed by a parent or in a family, which may or may not come with a belief.

In the book *Innovations and Elaborations in Internal Family Systems Therapy*, editors Martha Sweezy and Ellen L. Ziskind (2016), experts in Internal Family Systems Therapy, write about how covert legacy burdening is created by contagion because we are all capable of having feelings and absorbing beliefs without knowledge of their origins. Children, especially, are highly susceptible to their parents' feelings and beliefs. Likewise, Ann Sinko, a specialist in family therapies, describes covert legacy as free-floating internal states, energetic in nature, often experienced physiologically as anxiety, fear, and shame, feelings that have become disconnected from a story.

When we have no story to give a feeling of relational meaning, we're at greater risk of viewing ourselves as physically, morally, or psychologically defective. (Sinko, 2017, *Innovations and Elaborations in Internal Family Systems*) For example, as a therapist and educator, when I'm in a meeting with my supervisor, he may tell me to do something that goes against my personal beliefs or value system. I know that his directive doesn't make sense, nor will be beneficial to the work I am already doing. I know or believe that if I were to do as I have been told, it might lead to other behaviors that continue to go against my values, ethics, and beliefs. But instead of speaking up, I choose to remain silent and comply because of the power dynamics.

This experience reminds me of encounters I had with a parent or another person in authority (whom I feared). The expectation was that I would do what I was told and not question the instruction, especially because the other person had authority. I carried this burden throughout my life until I learned it is okay to question people in authority; there is a way of doing it without the fear of repercussions.

This is an example of a generational legacy burden connected to a shared belief that I learned at an early age: I was not to question anyone in authority.

Burdens can also be collective, originating from the group experience of one's ancestors, like genocide, slavery, famine, war, and so on. As I am writing this, our world is facing a pandemic, the coronavirus known as COVID-19. We are all experiencing the burdens of what this pandemic is placing upon us. Our anxieties are high due to economic downturns, the risk of contamination, and the burden of living our lives in ways we never imagined we would have to. This is a collective burden, which will eventually become a legacy. As mentioned earlier, a generational legacy is a thought, perspective, or belief system passed down from our families and communities via emotional and cultural pathways of communication, actions, and attitudes—whether conscious or unconscious. All of these live on in individuals and families and extend to other spheres of influence.

Many of us hold on to traumas we've experienced, even if we're not aware of them. These traumas are often held in our bodies, minds, hearts, souls, and spirits. What I have learned over the past several years is that the traumas my ancestors experienced can live on in me and are often manifested in my interactions with people who may activate, or "trigger," those traumatic experiences.

As Black people, we also regularly experience racial trauma, which can then lead to persistent traumatic stress. Recently, there has been a lot of talk and studies done about the concept of epigenetics. Epigenetics is the transferring of trauma across generations through the genes of an already traumatized person. Epigenetics tells us that post-traumatic stress disorder (PTSD) is a genetically inherited disorder, which can be passed down to offspring from either parent. (Burri et al., 2013) This is in line with the notion of intergenerational transmission of trauma and its connection to legacy burdens. For example, a pregnant woman with a traumatic past can impact the development of her growing fetus. The mother releases cortisol, which is absorbed by the baby via the placenta. This can have a huge impact on the baby's central nervous, automatic nervous, and limbic systems.

During this period of the pregnancy, the parent has difficulty or struggles to regulate her emotions. This can and may lead to a strained relationship between the mother and the child, and can or may also cause the inability to form a healthy attachment between the two. This, in turn, impacts the child's development and a sense of self over time with an inability to integrate experiences. Then later in life, the child, now an adult, is more prone to experience PTSD after a traumatic experience, struggles with relationships, unintentionally brings out negative behaviors in others, and is more emotionally detached. However, what we do know is that these behaviors can be transformed with treatment and support from mental health professionals. This healing can then impact future generations, thereby breaking the cycle of any legacy burdens.

As Black people, we tend to hold on to beliefs, thoughts, and behaviors even if they are killing us on the inside. Many of these beliefs, thoughts, and behaviors we learned during childhood. What we observed from our parents or caretakers, we understood as the only way to live or handle difficulties. These learned patterns of behaviors become hard to change or to let go of. Sometimes the problem is caused by what are known as "helicopter" or "overprotective" parents, parents who do not allow for breathing room between themselves and their children. These parents tend to hover over their children, overseeing every aspect of their children's lives. For example, a parent may teach her child how to ride a bike but is afraid to let the child pedal on her own. The child is not given the opportunity to fall and get back up and may be afraid of taking chances as an adult.

We may not have a clue as to where we inherited these beliefs, behaviors, or emotions, but they show up in multiple ways—in our relationships, our parenting, and our workplaces. A legacy burden is often found in feeling states, such as anxiety and fear. It is found in shared habits, such as smiling when we are angry, or in shared beliefs, such as distrust of the medical community. Our experiences of being abused (sexually, emotionally, or physically) or abandoned and rejected can then bring on burdens of shame, guilt, and emotional pain. These burdens are developed in families, which make them legacies that have been transmitted from one generation to the next.

The Role of Culture

Culture influences how we perceive, interpret, and express distress. Culture forms context as to how individuals and communities view and judge their responses to trauma. For example, if people think their communities would not accept them as victims or survivors, they may tend to withdraw and remain silent. This silence can be attributed to beliefs and thoughts associated with shame. They may internalize views, believing a traumatic experience is their fault.

We all belong to and are part of a culture or various cultures. Cultural factors influence our understanding of each other and how we see and connect to the world. Some aspects of our culture can be useful in helping us feel safe and connected to the world and the people around us. But we must also challenge ourselves when cultural beliefs and values hinder our growth. There can be a group of Black people in a room or at an event, and each one of them represents a different culture.

What is culture?

Culture is different from ethnicity. It includes the traditions, values, and customs (for instance, those transmitted through childcare and socialization practices) shared by a group of people. It includes rituals and artifacts that symbolize the group's belief system. It provides a psychic structure for social relationships and helps to create meaning in the physical world. Culture is learned and transmitted primarily through language and everyday interactions.

Furthermore, it is transmitted from generations to promote modifications and adaptations. A person's culture can be presented externally and represented internally. The external presentation is that of artifacts, roles, and institutions. The internal representation is composed of the values, beliefs, attitudes, cognitive style, epistemologies, and consciousness patterns that are shared within the group and passed from one generation to the next. We all can experience and express basic emotions (joy, fear, shame, guilt, disgust, sadness, etc.) no matter who we are or where we are from. The breakdown happens in how we perceive feelings based on cultural influences.

I earned my undergraduate degree from an HBCU. As an Afro-Caribbean, I remember well my struggles to fit in because I didn't grow up in the United States. I grew up listening to different music and in a different culture, and didn't understand some conversations because I didn't have historical context. I had to learn about Black people in America. As Caribbean people, at times we look down on Black Americans as though they are different from us. We pass judgment and quickly forget that we are perpetuating a system that sets us up to segregate ourselves. To make a difference, we must stop segregating ourselves, as the system had been so designed, and learn from each other to grow together, regardless of whether colonialism and racism took us to the Caribbean, the United States, or left us in Africa.

Types of Legacy Burdens

While researching materials to help me write this book, I came upon this quote by Dr. Judith Rich, a psychologist who changed her traditional practice into the mode of cultural transformation:

"If we break the chain of addiction, violence or other inherited, limiting beliefs, our children and their children and those who follow them are given access to possibilities not available to their ancestors. And thus, the entire lineage evolves." (Rich, Huffington Post 2011)

Perhaps you come from a lineage of addiction, people who found comfort in substance-based self-medication. Others may have a lineage of rage, violence, infidelity, and destructive behaviors to others and themselves. Maybe your legacy burdens are the weight of feeling like an outsider, like the "black sheep" seeking to belong. Indeed, regardless of heritage, your lineage may be a chain of survivors of many conflicts who are carriers of generational burdens that have been passed down and transferred onto you.

The Burden of Tradition and Culture

Tradition itself is not bad. It provides internal stability in the recurring acts in our daily lives, a certain routine and structure. It can help us stay connected with our roots. Hence, it is no surprise that tradition also plays an important part in religion, which is a major factor in how we interpret the moral standards that shape our identities. But there are dangers connected with tradition. Traditions grow over long periods, thus accumulating more and more details and aspects that were not originally part of God's word and plan. (Here I use the word "God" according to my own beliefs that I understand may be interpreted differently by others.) Think of the things you do as an individual and as a family that could be put under the label of tradition.

Knowing this helps us to understand that experiences are part of our human existence. They impact our feelings and thoughts in a powerful way. They shape the way we live our lives and how we interact with each other. However, experiences can also be deceiving in the same way that individual perceptions are. Each of us understands according to the personal experiences and legacies we inherit, as well as the ones we wish to create.

Cultural Wounding

Culture also influences how we perceive, interpret, and express distress. Culture forms the context of how individuals and communities view and judge their response to trauma and how individuals recognize trauma and are able to express it.

Family Burdens

As Black people, we are conditioned to respect our elders. Generations of Black families have grappled with the legacy of violence, colonialism, and racism due to the extreme economic inequality created by slavery and the continued dehumanizing that created a system in which Black people could not have equal political representation, own property, or fully access public goods and places, even common areas like parks and water fountains. The legacy burden is the violence rampant in Black and Brown communities due to the history of oppression, income instability, and the internalized (but often unrecognized) rage that occurs under these living conditions.

Familial violence occurs as individuals try to assert whatever power they have in these situations. But it's not uncommon for many Black and Brown families not to report any type of intimate-partner violence or sexual assault to law enforcement due to historical and institutional racism within law enforcement that has been held toward our communities. I know many women who refuse to call the police, and even when they do, choose not to press charges for the fear that their partner would end up in the criminal justice system—a system that has not been kind to Black men due to racial injustices. Many of these women may have observed these behaviors as a child either from their mothers or grandmothers and, therefore, choose to suffer in silence at the cost of their own safety.

These sufferings are often unspoken expectations, beliefs, and thoughts that later become burdens. There is a deep sense of loyalty to family. Within many families, there are the burdens of rage, rape, molestation, betrayal, theft, lies, and secrecy. These burdens keep many families in chains and bondage mentally. If only we could begin to see how these things can easily weigh us down and keep us from tapping into our true potential as human beings, we would be much better off, and so would our children and our grandchildren.

A new standard needs to be integrated into our parenting and home cultures, particularly around matters of gender expression and equality. We must incorporate healthy ways of communicating that help us acknowledge and talk about gender identification and beliefs about sexuality, dismantle secrecy, and remove the prohibition against speaking about the past or unpleasant things like sexual abuse. We must invite the expression of emotions, reset unspoken values, and establish healthy child-rearing practices that promote emotional and mental health and safety.

Trauma is deeply rooted in the Black community. When people are traumatized, they can't help but blame the past and, at the same time, inflict trauma on their own children. It's not always the same *kind* of trauma, so the nature of the transmission can be subtle. This is what we call multi-generational transmission. In family therapy, there's a saying: "It takes three generations to heal." The first generation inflicts the trauma, the next generation gets into recovery, and, hopefully, the third generation is spared. It moves from *infliction* to *healing* to *release*. The multi-generational trauma flows on and on, an endless river of hurt and pain.

Financial Burdens

On May 28 and June 1, 1921, a mob of White residents attacked Black residents and businesses in the Greenwood District of Tulsa, Oklahoma. At that time, the Greenwood District was the wealthiest Black community in the United States, known as "Black Wall Street." It had one of the highest concentrations of Black-owned businesses in the country even though segregation restricted African American housing choices and prohibited Black customers from patronizing businesses that catered to only White customers. Black Wall Street was a vibrant African American neighborhood with a thriving middle class and well-established institutions like schools, churches, and civic associations. The attack robbed many Blacks of their wealth and their opportunity to leave their families a financial legacy.

As Black people with limited to no resources, many of us have not been taught good financial management. We grew up in families and communities where we saw our parents and our friends' parents struggling to keep the family financially afloat. Our parents often worked more than one job to financially provide for the family. As children, we were witnesses to our parents and other family members' financial pressures. Therefore, we have become slaves to credit and burdened by debt.

The "slave to credit" mentality becomes burdensome in that we no longer see the benefit of creating a financial legacy for future generations. Our relationship with money becomes more of a means to an end rather than a process by which we need to build financial stability. Our limiting beliefs around abundance and money is another burden. Slavery taught Black people resilience but not the means to prosperity. Therefore, measures of rising out of poverty vary.

According to the Urban Institute, slightly more than half of all Americans enter poverty at some time in their lives. Blacks, Latinx, households headed by women, and those with lower levels of education are more likely to become poor. Some who get out of poverty will cycle into poverty again within five years. (McKernan, Ratcliffe, and Cellini, 2009) Many social scientists estimate that it takes three to five generations for a family's wealth or poverty to dissipate, but others, including economic historian Gregory Clark, have stated that the move takes ten to fifteen generations (see the interview in The New Republic 2014). The COVID pandemic and its disproportionate impact on lower-income Black communities, due to the economic impact of segregation, skews the financial inequality even greater.

Today, in 2021, the net worth of the average Black family is about one-eighth that of the average White family, based on data from the US Bureau of Labor Statistics. Much of that difference derives from the value of the family's residence. Houses in areas where predominantly White people live sell for much more than those in areas where there are Black, Hispanic, or integrated neighborhoods. So power, wealth, and advantage—or lack thereof—are passed down from parent to child. For this reason, wealth isn't just luxury or profit; it's the starting point for the next generation.

A PBS series on race broadcast in 2003 gave this summation for Episode 3, The House We Live In: "New studies reveal that when the 'family wealth gap' between Blacks and Whites is considered, there is no difference in test scores, graduation rates, welfare usage, and other measures. It's a lack of opportunities, not natural differences, that is responsible for continuing inequality." Wealth, more than any other measure, shows the accumulated impact of past discrimination and shapes an individual's chances in life.

Health and Mental Health Burdens

Black people are less likely to seek treatment, or to be compliant with treatment recommendations, because they have been dealing with a healthcare system that has mistreated them for years. Multiple high-profile events have affirmed and reaffirmed their belief about a healthcare system rooted in racial hatred that continues to shape many Black people's approaches to healthcare. This belief is rooted in the history of the United States' long legacy of discriminating against and exploiting Black Americans. The memory of these atrocities remains deeply embedded in the fabric and the collective consciousness of the community.

Who doesn't remember the Tuskegee Syphilis Experiment of 1932? The Tuskegee study was designed to document the natural history of syphilis. What they did, though, was *not* treat the 600 mostly poor, illiterate Blacks who were already infected and intentionally did not disclose to these men that their condition was treatable. Additionally, in 1973, in the Relf Sisters Sterilization case, doctors used a federally funded clinic to illegally and permanently sterilize two young sisters, ages 12 and 14. They did this as a method to control the population of Black people throughout the impoverished South.

In the pre–Civil War South, the use of enslaved people for medical research was equally common. Dr. J. Marion Sims, known as the "father of gynecology," believing that Black women didn't feel as much pain as White women, experimented on countless enslaved pregnant Black women without anesthesia to establish his professional reputation. Not all our ancestors survived his brutal experiments.

Even during the coronavirus pandemic (COVID-19), we still see the exploitation of Black people by racist doctors. It was reported that two French doctors divulged their desire to test coronavirus vaccines on African people, comparing them to sex workers who "don't protect themselves" to justify their racist proposal. Therefore, many Blacks continue not to trust our healthcare system and the medical community today.

Furthermore, in the field of mental health, the psychiatric diagnosis of drapetomania, or "runaway slave syndrome," was created to diagnose and pathologize African slaves who fled their vicious slave owners. Slaves who ran away were considered diseased and were treated with amputation of extremities. Later, White Americans argued that former slaves would not thrive in a free society because their minds could not psychologically manage freedom.

As a result of these systemic burdens, many Blacks have been taught to keep their business and feelings to themselves. If you're Black in this culture, there's a long and difficult history of penalization and demonization for expressing how you feel. This belief has been passed down from generation to generation. You learn that silence, even amid facing insufferable pain and terror, is the only way to protect yourself. If you break that silence, disclosing any hurt to anyone—sometimes even to your closest friends and family members —it is considered a sign of weakness. To break that code of silence is unacceptable and unimaginable. Among many Black people, disclosure is difficult because the same oppressive and brutal system our ancestors were warned about still exists today. Caution to maintain silence protects us from the harshness. Thus, we adopt this belief: "don't trust anyone; don't you dare trust a soul."

The fear of punishment, judgment, and backlash runs deep for many Blacks. We have this belief that if we hold in our feelings and thoughts, our suffering will go away. Asking for help is not the foremost thought on our minds. To confide in anyone but God is considered a no-no. As Blacks, we may battle with constant thoughts such as, *What will happen to me if I admit I'm scared, depressed, alone, hurting, or anxious? Who can I trust to share my secrets and thoughts with? Is there anyone who will not judge me?* Whenever I mention the idea of therapy to a friend or person of color, there's almost always a response of resistance. When I talk to my Christian Black friends about therapy, the first response I get is, "I pray; I go to God, and He is the only one I need to talk to." My thought is, *Then why are you talking to me?* However, I do understand where this thinking comes from.

Often, we receive help from someone who doesn't look like us and can't relate to our stories or our experiences. We are often not heard because the listener cannot connect to (or identify with) our problems. Still, the ability to relate to one another helps us feel understood and helps us to heal. That is not easy to do, especially if we are already branded by conceptions *or misconceptions* about who we are before we even open our mouths.

Silence, we think, also protects those around us. Case in point, on June 7, 2020, my family lost the youngest of ten siblings to pancreatic cancer. To say that this was a shock would be minimizing the impact of his death on the family. Not only was his death a surprise, but news of his diagnosis unexpected.

It was during the height of COVID that his health took a turn for the worse. At the time we had no idea he was that ill. He had gone to Panama with my husband on vacation in early 2020 and seemed to be doing well. However, two months after he returned from his vacation, he started to complain about not feeling well and being weak and exhausted. Due to the rise in COVID rates, we all thought he had the virus and encouraged him to get tested. I'm not sure if he did or not before his hospitalization.

In May 2020, his symptoms of respiratory issues started. He complained about having difficulty breathing. One of my older sisters told his wife that if she didn't take him to the emergency room, she would call 911 and have an ambulance come get him. You see, at the time, my brother was living in Savannah, Georgia and was the primary caretaker of my 93-year-old mother, who lived with him and his wife. I assume he opted to go to the hospital rather than have an ambulance arrive at the house because he didn't want my mother to know what was happening. An ambulance would have alerted her to how sick he was. A few weeks before, she had reported that she had not seen him in days, even though they lived in the same home.

My brother was admitted to the hospital sometime between May 5 and May 8. It's all a blur, the same as when my father died, and I still have the impulse to block painful events—*no woman, no cry*. Once admitted, he was tested for COVID, and we were assured that it was not the coronavirus. We were relieved. However, he was given oxygen to help with his breathing. Each day that passed, we would check in on him via family group text, asking for updates. He assured us he was getting better and would be discharged soon. We waited for his discharge date, but it never came. He didn't get discharged as he had told us he would and was placed back on oxygen. Yet he continued to assure us, via text messages, that he was getting better.

Several weeks went by, and he was still in the hospital. I started to get worried, and every time I asked about his health, he reported that he was getting better and awaiting his discharge date. He continued to tell us he was dealing with just respiratory problems and was waiting for the okay to be discharged. Still, it didn't seem right. And then it happened. The call came from his wife, letting me know that the hospital had called. His organs were shutting down, and they were taking him to another unit.

Honestly, I can't even remember what my sister-in-law said because all I heard was "organs shutting down" and that he had "Stage 2 pancreatic cancer." I dropped the phone, speechless. I couldn't think; this was not making any sense. How could he go from respiratory difficulties to pancreatic cancer in a matter of three weeks? This was not happening. This could not be true. After hanging up with her, I called each of my siblings to give them the news: our brother was fighting for his life.

I immediately searched online. I needed to quickly learn the prognosis of Stage 2 pancreatic cancer. I acted like a madwoman, trying to find out anything and everything about this wretched disease. I learned it was one of the most difficult cancers to detect early. If not caught early, the chance of survival was low. I also learned that at Stage 2, the chances of survival were between 13% and 39%—at least five years—depending on where the cancer was located in the body. I didn't have enough information about its location, but I built my hope on the 39% and five years. I felt better with this news. I knew there was hope.

I imagined my siblings were all doing their own research as well. As a praying family, we started to pray for his survival. His wife sent us updates about his progress, for instance, reporting that he was responding to simple commands. Though I was appreciative of the positive updates, something still didn't feel right. There was this feeling of unsettledness. She would report that he could wiggle his toes, squeeze the nurses' hands, and so forth. But the thought kept bothering me, *How could he not know that he was that sick? Did he not know that he had cancer? How did we not know that he was sicker than what he led us to believe?* We were a family who texted each other every day, and he always ending his text messages with the words "GIVE THANKS" all in caps.

One week after I had received the call that his organs were shutting down, my brother lost his battle with cancer. This was quite a traumatic experience for all of us. Our 93-year-old mother outlived the youngest child of the family. It was devastating.

It wasn't until the last few hours of his life that we learned from his attending physician that he had received a diagnosis of *Stage 4* pancreatic cancer three days into his hospitalization and was informed that his prognosis for survival was very slim to none. You can imagine my feelings of betrayal, knowing that my brother understood all along that he would not make it. I didn't even get to spend time with him. Yet, I also thought of how isolated, lonely, and scared he must have felt there in the hospital, especially amid a pandemic, where he could not have visitors. Although he never told his children, and he never told us either, we do believe he told his wife.

As I sit here writing this section, I think of the burden he was carrying. The burden of his health issues. The secrecy about his illness. His unwillingness to seek medical attention when he was not feeling well. The shame he must have been carrying about having cancer. His own beliefs about the healthcare system. The many things he heard or observed from my father about medical treatment and the healthcare system. I thought of my father, who also kept his kidney problems a secret from the family. He loathed and didn't trust the healthcare system to provide proper health care. It wasn't until my father became ill and was hospitalized and placed on dialysis that we knew the seriousness of his kidney disease and his diagnosis of multiple myeloma, a type of cancer that affects plasma cells, which can cause kidney problems. However, we had several years with my father before he passed.

Black men's health is important, but because of the history of Blacks and the medical healthcare systems, they do not trust those systems. So many Blacks carry the burdens of pushing through with health problems and opt not to get medical treatment. This thinking is common within the Caribbean community as well. I have had conversations with many friends and family members who were ill or received diagnoses about severe medical issues but chose not to receive medical attention or inform their families of their illness. This is a burden we must release as a people. We must let go of the beliefs and shame we carry about health and medical illnesses and choose not to pass it down to the next generation. We must encourage them to be vulnerable, seek help, and ask for support. But, again, asking for help is not the foremost thought on Black people's minds.

According to Mental Health America (MHA), communities of color historically experience unique and considerable challenges in accessing mental health services. To me, it seems as though mental health issues are more prevalent in Black communities than we are willing to admit. To concede that we have mental health issues is to own guilt and deal with shame and all kinds of heavy feelings—opening Pandora's box. We would experience many emotional processes, which we have not been taught or trained to cope with and manage. Here are some demographic and societal issues faced by many Blacks, according to MHA:

- 13.2% of the US population, or roughly 45.7 million people, identify themselves as Black or African American, according to 2014 US Census Bureau numbers. Another 2.5% identified as multiracial. This represents an increase from 12.6% who identified themselves as Black/African American in the 2010 Census.

- As of 2010, 55% of all Black/African American people lived in the South, 18% lived in the Midwest, 17% in the Northeast, and 10% in the West.

Historical adversity, which includes slavery, sharecropping, and race-based exclusion from health, educational, social, and economic resources, translates into socioeconomic disparities experienced by African Americans today. Socioeconomic status, in turn, is linked to mental health: People who are impoverished, homeless, incarcerated, or have substance abuse problems are at higher risk for poor mental health.

Despite progress made over the years, racism continues to impact the mental health of Blacks/African Americans. Negative stereotypes and social rejection have decreased but continue to occur with measurable, adverse consequences. Historical and contemporary instances of negative treatment have led to a distrust of authorities, many of whom Blacks/African Americans see as not having their best interests in mind. (Mental Health America 2014)

Here are statistics from the US Health and Human Services Office of Minority Health:

- In the 2019 National Survey on Drug and Alcohol Use and Health, adult Blacks/African Americans were 20% more likely to report serious psychological distress in the past year than adult Whites.
- Blacks/African Americans living below the poverty line are three times more likely to report serious psychological distress than those living above poverty.
- Adult Blacks/African Americans are more likely to have feelings of sadness, hopelessness, and worthlessness than are adult Whites.

- While Blacks/African Americans are less likely than White people to die from suicide as teenagers, Blacks/African American teenagers are more likely to attempt suicide than are White teenagers (8.3% vs. 6.2%). (Office of Minority Mental Health 2016)

Note that the statistics above were gathered through collaborations and partnership organizations such as the Capstone Institute/Center for Research on the Education of Students Placed at Risk, Howard University, and the National Black Nurses Association, whose specific aim was outreach to Black/African Americans, given the reluctance of Blacks to seek help on their own. Note also that Blacks are overrepresented in prisons (13% of the general population but nearly 40% of the prison population), which may influence the survey answers.

Educational Burdens

Education disparity still exists today in this country, and it's nothing new. Unfortunately, the education system in America is not set up so that many Black and Brown families in this country benefit from it— nor has it ever been. Let's look at educational inequality.

When you think about it, the difficulty is not only providing equal distribution of academic resources, which include school funding and qualified and experienced teachers, but also not having enough resources such as books and the technologies needed to provide a good and decent education. We tend to find educational inequalities in historically disadvantaged and oppressed communities. However, the most salient issue is that of funding. In fact, it's one of the biggest issues facing the American public education system. In this system, at least 90% of the K–12 school educational funding comes from state and local governments, largely generated by sales, property, and income tax. Therefore, where a person lives will determine the amount of funding their local schools receive. If you live in a suburban neighborhood where taxes are higher and people within that neighborhood have higher incomes, the educational institutions in that area will have access to more resources.

The other impact influencing educational burdens is the structural inequality that exists within our educational system. What is structural inequality? Marginalized children must attend public schools, while rich children can attend private schools. Another factor is that females are oftentimes guided to take certain types of courses or pursue certain career fields different from the types of professions many males are guided toward, such as the engineering or medical fields.

The question is this: why is it important to speak up about structural inequality and disparities in education? Many of the educational challenges that burden Black communities exist because these of structural qualities and the disparity in education. Therefore, it is important that as parents, we take an active role in how and where our children are educated. Too often you might hear many parents, especially within Black communities, tell their children that they, their spouse, or their own parents didn't go to high school. When our children hear and receive these messages, they often don't see the value of education (or even higher education) because there are no role models who show them its importance.

How do we address these burdens given that in the past African American and Blacks did not have equal opportunity to quality education and were not valued by educators as being worthy to be educated?

Young Blacks are oftentimes criticized by others in the community. "Why are you trying to get a White man's education?" they are asked. Although this statement can have different meanings, it is often not explained so that the young person can understand it or where it stems from.

In 2018 the United Negro College Fund's (UNCF) Frederick D. Patterson's Research Institute issued a report regarding a study of 797 youth living in households with an annual income of $40,000. The Institute identified educational challenges:

- African American youths report more difficulty in school success because of lack of financial resources, concerns with standardized testing, and limited support.
- More than one-third of African American youths believe their race will limit their opportunities.
- Only 43% reported feeling safe at their schools.

("African American Leaders Unhappy with K-12 Education System; Eager to Make Changes" n.d.)

Spiritual and Religious Burdens

"It ran in your family until it ran into you. God says you've been anointed to break the cycle. Generational curses stop with you." ~ Popular Faith Quote

There's no way as a Black Christian woman that I can write a book without including some aspect of spirituality. I grew up in what I would call a semi-Christian home because my dad wasn't so much of a "Christian" or "religious person," but he made sure we went to church with my mom every week without fail. How could I write this book and not include something about religion or spirituality and how it has impacted my life? Certain religious beliefs started to burden me, and I had to unpack them and even some of the values I had learned. I needed to do that to release myself of those burdens so that I too can have a better relationship not only with myself but also with God.

As we know, religion and spirituality are the first go-to's for many Blacks, in part because they are more accessible than professional mental healthcare. Historically, religion was a source of relief for enslaved people—first, their own faith practices, which often included healing arts, song, and dance, then (as these were stripped from them) Christianity, which provided a gathering place for support and sometimes rebellion. This is a legacy that can, at times, become a burden.

Mental health and wellness are important and ignored too often in the Black community because many have been conditioned to believe that all they need is Jesus. We fail to remember that His help comes from a variety of sources, and seeing a mental health therapist is one of them. We are often told to give everything over to God, and, yes, I agree that's where you should start. However, we can also believe and have faith that God will help, and there's no question that He won't. He will help to heal your soul, even the deeply rooted places of your soul where the spirit resides. Nevertheless, He doesn't want us to suffer either. Going to therapy with a mental health professional who respects your faith practice is what He would want you to do. We must remember that Jesus was a counselor, and many went to Him for guidance.

Having said that, where did the reluctance to seek mental health counseling come from? As stated earlier, Black communities have a distrust of medical and mental health services and, perhaps more importantly, feel shame in admitting to what they perceive as weakness—particularly outside of the Black community. Based on my experience, personally and as a therapist, Black men tend to view their role as masculine—confident, assertive, and hard-working. They value living in an interconnected community and cultivating interpersonal relationships. Black women, on the other hand, view their role as being hard-working, independent, mentally and emotionally resilient, and nurturing. They feel as though they must embody both masculine and feminine traits. This is perhaps a legacy from being enslaved, when women were forced into labor and at the same time needed to care for their children. It could also be from the conditioning of one's belief that "you don't need a man," which might stem from the trauma associated with abandonment, whether by choice or by instruction. If the husband was sold off to another plantation against his will, crops still needed tending, chores still needed to be done, and children still needed their mama.

As a first-generation Black college student with high expectations placed on me, I know how hard it is to ask for help. Let me again remind you that when I found out my father had died, I didn't cry. I called my clinical supervisor for guidance on counseling the clients I had scheduled. It took a lot of therapy and conversation with colleagues for me to understand the burdens I was carrying and how I might release them—all while maintaining the Christian spiritual faith I grew up with.

"FINDING YOURSELF" IS NOT REALLY HOW IT WORKS. YOU AREN'T A TEN-DOLLAR BILL IN LAST WINTER'S COAT POCKET. YOU ARE ALSO NOT LOST. YOUR TRUE SELF IS RIGHT THERE, BURIED UNDER CULTURAL CONDITIONING, OTHER PEOPLE'S OPINIONS, AND INACCURATE CONCLUSIONS YOU DREW AS A KID THAT BECAME YOUR BELIEFS ABOUT WHO YOU ARE. "FINDING YOURSELF" IS ACTUALLY RETURNING TO YOURSELF. AN UNLEARNING, AN EXCAVATION, A REMEMBERING WHO YOU WERE BEFORE THE WORLD GOT ITS HANDS ON YOU.
EMILY McDOWELL

Chapter 4

Decolonize Your Mind, Body, and Spirit

"Emancipate yourself from mental slavery."

~Bob Marley

Our ancestors who suffered slavery knew the barriers that separated them from freedom. They were reminded of them every day of their lives. They saw it from the moment they woke up in their squalid living conditions. Most of their accommodations were homes built of wood or earth with no foundations. A few lived in buildings with actual frames and masonry, but usually these structures had served another previous purpose and were refitted for Blacks to dwell in.

Plenty of slaves also had no accommodations at all and were instructed to sleep where they worked, be it in the kitchen, the stable, or the laundry room of a house. In other words, they were told, "You have no home but what we give you, and sometimes not even that."

Nutrition was a barrier between slaves and a normal life as well. They were told what to eat, where to eat it, and when. If they didn't like what was served or weren't hungry, they simply didn't eat. Over time, many were brainwashed into believing they should be thanking those who enslaved them for feeding them, despite the spartan servings and poor quality of the meals.

Lack of education was another barrier, which was not as obvious but nonetheless present. In addition to slaves being strictly kept from learning to read to prevent any uprising that would disrupt the economy and put the lives of their masters in peril, the most omnipotent barrier for our ancestors was the learned knowledge that not obeying the commands of their 'owners' 24 hours a day for the rest of their lives would be met with repercussions—from starvation to physical punishment to execution. Every slave, whether they worked on a dangerous sugar plantation or as a maid in the governor's mansion, faced the same barriers to freedom each and every day of their lives.

Modern Barriers to Healing

While Black, indigenous, and other people of color (BIPOC) no longer live as slaves in the United States, the barriers separating us from true freedom, healing, and good mental health still exist. We must rethink our inherited belief system as well as challenge the worldview placed upon us if we are to break free from the invisible shackles that continue to tie us down and hold us in place.

Other people's belief systems and even our own do not necessarily reflect the truth, but time and prejudice have allowed them to remain in place. Malaise, a lack of belief in our right to better days, and a lack of education on how to achieve what we want all contribute to the challenges of Black people unable to break free from the limitations imposed on their ancestors during slavery.

It starts in our education system from the moment we enter the public school system. When we begin to take history courses, we usually learn about events that happened around the time of the European Crusades—when White men used the sword to take Christianity to the 'savage, unwashed lands' of the Muslim world and Northern Africa. From there, we cover significant events in Europe, such as the Battle of Hastings, King Henry VIII's establishment of the Church of England, the defeat of the Spanish Armada, the signing of the Magna Carta, and the long, winding succession of European explorers who took to the sea and slowly but surely 'discovered' North and South America. (But there were a lot of struggles for power between the various ruling entities of Europe, even in religion.)

What of African history during this time? Anthropology tells us that the first modern humans evolved in East Africa 200,000 years ago, but men like Christopher Columbus, who enslaved the first people he saw upon reaching North America, are revered with holidays. During the Middle Ages, there were up to 10,000 different states active on the African continent, but in the pages of our children's history books, Africa gets an early mention for the prowess of the ancient Egyptians who built their pyramids and the Sphinx, then isn't mentioned again until discussions about the European slave trade of the 15th century that first brought BIPOC to what would later become the United States.

Our educational system tells only of the exploits of White inventors and forward thinkers—of Isaac Newton and Thomas Edison and Albert Einstein. Alice Parker, who invented central heating... Charles Richard Drew, who deduced how to preserve blood plasma for a length of time... Granville T. Woods, who has almost sixty railroad patents... and Percy Lavon Julian, who created the drug physostig-mine, which is used to treat glaucoma, cannot be found in most Amer-ican history books. It's not just in our education system either. Watch any news broadcast for 30 minutes, and you'll see reports on the White leaders of White countries (i.e., US, England, and Canada) being propped up to be the be-all and end-all of world politics. If Africa is mentioned at all, it's usually because of a flood or famine resulting in the massive loss of life.

The Inner Struggle

While the outside world of the United States has a significant Euro-centric tilt to it, Black people's own internal beliefs are even more of an issue that separates them from mental health and freedom. Passing down unhealthy beliefs, actions, and traditions keeps us from achieving a better life for ourselves. Our mistrust of others limits our ability to form healthy relationships. Our ideas about medicine, psychology, and counseling limit our thought processes when it comes to dealing with internal struggles. These are burdens too heavy a load to carry.

Who do we see when we look in the mirror? Do we define ourselves on our own terms, or does someone else's definition come to mind first? Do we see ourselves as equal to anyone else in the world, worthy, having the capacity to give and receive love, and a contributing member of society capable of anything we put our minds to? The sad, short answer for many is "no."

Most often, we see ourselves as limited before we even have a chance to explore all that we are and could become. Limited by the color of our skin. Limited by our lack of family finances. Perhaps limited by our fractured family unit, as divorce rates are higher for Blacks than for Whites at every age. We see ourselves as limited to the neighbor-hood we live in, where few seem to leave and move to something better. We see ourselves as limited by our opportunities as an adult, with college being viewed as either not needed or not possible, while living paycheck to paycheck is more common. When we achieve success, we may feel limited by the views of our family and friends that perhaps we've "sold out" to climb the social ranks.

This limited self-awareness, which exists both externally and internally, cripples our ability to experience healthy emotions, think creatively, and perform actions that will better our lives, and crushes our ability to practice self-love. We feel we haven't earned it and don't deserve it, and it twists our thought process to where we convince ourselves we don't need those things.

This concept feeds into the Black person's notion of strength. We envision the stereotypical strong, proud Black woman—quick to anger, fiercely loyal to her family and closest friends, battling against prejudice, both perceived and real, every day of her life. She is unable to relax or explore life and different mindsets beyond her current set of circumstances and the ingrained beliefs of what life is about that she learned from her mother and older siblings and relatives.

The stereotypical strong, silent Black man suffers from similar incorrect beliefs. His value comes from hard work—tireless labor without complaint, without taking a sick day, doing whatever it takes to ensure there is money on the table for clothes, shoes, food, and a roof over his family's head. His emotional health is a black hole. If his father smoked, drank, gambled, used drugs, or cheated on his spouse, he is likely to endure similar vices, even if he witnessed those things and their negative impacts as a child. He avoids doctors because he fears what they might say, rather than trusting their ability to fix his body. The idea of talking about his feelings or emotions is so foreign it never even crosses his mind. Such things don't matter in his mindset. As long as he has a job to go to in the morning and a paycheck at the end of each week, he is fulfilling his role as husband and father.

What we now know is that denying parts of ourselves denies us the opportunity to break free of the barriers that are limiting us from experiencing the true pantheon of the human experience. We do not consider the idea of questioning the beliefs that have been passed on to us from previous generations and from the Eurocentric society we live in. By doing so, we are limiting our ability to heal from past trauma inflicted on our ancestors and genetically carried down through the years. The opportunity to learn, embrace, and take on multiple worldviews evades us because we have contributed to our own status of wearing blinders at all times. We cannot find the solutions to our problems because we aren't even willing to admit that those problems exist, and in many cases, we are completely unaware of them.

Stigmas About Mental Health Black People Believe

One of the most potent and debilitating taboos remaining in communities of BIPOC is that of mental illness, specifically its discussion, self-concern, the idea of needing help, and admitting to thoughts of depression, anxiety, or suicide. Therapists and psychologists are often not viewed as real doctors but as scam artists and charlatans who exist only to separate BIPOC from their money. Because of socioeconomic conditions, it is highly likely that many more BIPOC are suffering from mental health conditions than those who report those negative feelings. Consider the following:

- In the United States, 39% of African American children and teenagers are living in poverty, compared with 14% of White and Asian children and teenagers.
- Minority racial groups are more likely to experience poverty passed from one generation to the next than Whites.
- African Americans (53%) are more likely to receive high-cost mortgages than Whites (18%).
- African American unemployment rates are usually double that of Whites. African American men working full-time

earn only about 72% of the average White man in the same position.

Any or all of these statistics could easily lead a person of any race to heightened feelings of stress, despair, anger, or anxiety. Even such luminary Black leaders as Dr. Martin Luther King, Jr. reportedly suffered from severe depression but waved off psychiatric care, even as members of his own inner circle begged him to get help. In times of slavery, White owners held the misconception that slaves were not sophisticated enough to develop mental health disorders, and such mental states were explained away as fatigue or laziness. This leads many in the BIPOC communities to view mental health as being a 'White thing,' that is, a sign of weakness.

Research indicates that Blacks develop mental health conditions as much as any other ethnic group but seek care far less often. Only 25% of Blacks pursue it compared with 40% of Whites, despite the frequent presence of traumatic stressors. Religious beliefs also often keep Blacks from pursuing traditional medical-based mental health solutions. Blacks will often want to rely solely on their spiritual and religious communities, the power of prayer, the words of their religious leaders, and the support from the Black Church as all the help they need to deal with any struggles. While these can all be vital components in recovery from trauma, with the exception of prayer, they all negate the important focus on the individual and dealing with their internal beliefs and misconceptions that are causing feelings of depression, anxiety, anger, stress, and so on.

Without proper avenues of release and coping strategies for these mental struggles, we end up internalizing them, which affects many components of our day-to-day lives and how we process the things we see, do, and feel, along with how we receive information based on how we self-identify and the experiences that have shaped our mindset and belief systems.

BIPOC Stigmas in Relation to Upbringing and Conditioning

Our stigmas do not develop overnight. They are cultivated over a lifetime of experiences, teachings from our paternal figures and other role models, our experience with other population groups who label us as BIPOC, and what we learn from the Eurocentric world around us.

Racism is a significant component of our internalization. It can manifest in completely different ways for any two people, even two people in the same family who grew up in the same household. For some, it brings a deflated sense of self, confidence, and/or power. They see how Black people are treated by the police, by certain government offices, and by those in a higher social or economic stratum, and they feel defeated internally without ever uttering a single word. At the opposite end of the spectrum, other people develop an overinflated sense of confidence or authority. Despite their own personal shortcomings—lack of steady employment, a formal education, or material things that traditionally signify success in life, such as a home or a car—they project an attitude of complete control over their surroundings, dismissing others' claims that they could improve their lives. Both of these are directly related to the concept of otherness—the circumstance by which a dominant group (us) stigmatizes a second group (them) based on a real or imagined difference.

Intentionally downgrading Black people's value based on their skin pigment is the most obvious example of this, with other groups using it as a discriminatory weapon. This leads to a struggle with a sense of belonging; many BIPOC feel comfortable interacting with only people who look like them because they have bought into the prejudice that comes from groups making the repetitive assumption that Black skin equates to negative characteristics.

This also leads Black people to fall prey to the consequences of identity politics, techniques used to diminish the power of Black voters as they were used during Reconstruction and throughout the 160 years since the end of the Civil War. Diminishing potential Black voting blocs through the divide-and-conquer tactic has been used repeatedly throughout history. Blacks are told their votes don't matter as much; they fear losing income or their jobs if they exercise their right to vote during the workday, and the location, hours, and procedure of polling centers are often not well-advertised in Black communities.

Negative Effects of Internalization

Internalization can have long-lasting effects that significantly damage our mental health, hurting our self-image, relationships, and ability to succeed and achieve happiness long term. By not dealing with negative experiences, learned beliefs, and external instances of prejudice and otherness, we set ourselves up for future triggering and trauma from events, even after years or decades. The simple fact is that if incidents are not dealt with mentally, they will stay with us. Our brains are not a city dump where bad thoughts are tossed into a heap and forgotten; nor are they places where we can bury our fears and wounds and never worry about hearing from them again. All it takes is a certain stimulus, internal or external, and the trauma can seem as real as when it actually happened, disrupting our lives significantly and repeatedly until it is finally dealt with.

Internalization can also cause us to stay silent instead of sharing experiences with loved ones, or to avoid seeking treatment, even if we suspect it could have a tremendous impact on improving our health. These feelings of diminished importance and worthlessness lead us to believe that we are not meant to feel better or that we should not waste our friends' and family's time complaining about our own feelings. We think back to our role models from childhood and remember their stoic attitudes, stiff upper lips, and refusal to let anything impede their choices to exist.

Even if we thought our role models were unhappy, and that in turn made us unhappy as children, we often cannot see the connection from one to the other and continue to emulate our parents' poor choices and lack of self-care. All of these decisions result in self-sabotaging the healing we desperately need. We might think we are taking the right path by putting others' needs before our own in all circumstances. We either cannot admit or do not realize that when we refuse to help ourselves, over time we are damaging our ability to help others.

I personally learned this the hard way. I was too busy helping others and neglected to take care of my own emotional needs. I neglected the parts of me I was too afraid to examine and confront. I learned over time that it doesn't have to be that way; I can take care of my emotional and mental health as a way to help others take care of theirs.

Developing Self-Help Tools

No matter what steps we take, we won't feel 100% better overnight, but by using techniques and educating ourselves, we can slowly start the healing process. The following actions are suggestions you can take to begin discovering your true identity, unlocking the trauma of racism and slavery that are controlling you unconsciously, and learning what self-love and self-care look like.

Giving Yourself Permission

- This is such a simple act we struggle so mightily with. Starting from a place of quiet meditation, give yourself permission to:
- Reclaim an Africanist worldview, setting aside the Eurocentric view that has pervaded your life since childhood.
- Develop an attitude of self-empowerment and cultivate an environment that supports that. Don't let others decide what you are capable of. Discover it for yourself.
- Learn the history of White supremacy and realize that many of the restraints and disconnects you may feel from other populations are rooted in that discriminatory landscape and the echoes of slavery.
- Make the promise to yourself to stop limiting what you feel, experience, accept, and acknowledge about your own humanity. Step out of the life you know to take on new experiences, to spend time with different segments of the population, to travel, to try different activities, and to open your mind to new ways of thinking besides what has been instilled in you since birth.

Unconscious Conditioned Thoughts and Forms of Communication

The Unconscious Thought Theory (UTT) suggests that the unconscious mind is capable of performing actions without a person's awareness based on previous stimulants or patterns of learned behavior. For a Black person, this could manifest in many ways. For example, we may immediately feel guilty when we see a police car driving behind us, even though we've done nothing wrong. We may not apply for a well-paying job because we think only White people should make so much money.

The way we communicate often diminishes our meaning, how we are perceived, and the way we think about ourselves. Areas to watch and make conscious decisions to improve on include:

- **Subtlety of Communication:** These include chemical signals, tactile signals, auditory signals, and visual signals. They are the emotions and attitudes we give off without saying a single word. If we are sweaty from work and bleary from a lack of sleep when we sit down to lecture a child or try to persuade a spouse to purchase something, our message may be interpreted differently.
- **Tone:** When we use a harsh tone of voice with others, they become defensive and cast us as angry, aggressive, or stressed. A harsh tone in Blacks is often a by-product of their upbringing and tied directly to slavery, where 'tough love' was the order of the day for Black parents dealing with their own children. It might have maintained order, but it utterly lacked empathy.
- **Verbal Language:** Using certain language comes directly from uncomfortable times in our past—colonization, patriarchy, etc. When you use words that come from a history of racism, White supremacy, and slavery, you view those words as acceptable in your own vernacular and diminish the wrongness that should pervade them in the mind of any civilized adult.
- **Body Language and Self-Awareness:** What does your posture say? How about the way you set your feet and how you sit? Are you shrinking away from conversations, fearing

criticism? Are you aggressively leaning forward, expecting a discussion to turn into a confrontation?

- **Black Men's Tendency to Occupy Space:** Black men often seek to assert their dominance over others by taking up more space than is necessary, both in a physical environment or in a conversation. "Manspreading" is the practice where a man, particularly onboard public transportation such as a subway or bus, will sit with his legs spread wide apart to ward off anyone seeking to sit in a nearby seat. He might also use an adjacent seat as a footrest, even if it takes away space for another person to sit. In conversation, the term "mansplaining" refers to the process by which a man explains a situation to someone he looks down on, often a woman, by using language and tone that are meant to be patronizing or condescending.

- **Black Women's Tendency to Shrink:** At the opposite end of the spectrum are the tendencies of Black women to avoid confrontation, particularly with men. Whether it's in the classroom, the office meeting, or in a 1:1 relationship, women will doubt their own abilities to offer knowledge and solve problems, even if it results in them being perceived as unintelligent. Similarly, they will seek to remain as still and small as possible to limit the possibility of being singled out or ridiculed.

- **Alignment of Words:** It's not just what you say. It's how you say it and what actions you take while you're saying it. If you tell your boss you will stay late tonight to finish up work as you busily type on your keyboard, you will be viewed as a dedicated worker. If you say the same thing with your arms folded as you stare out the window, you'll be viewed negatively. The message might be the same to you, but perception can make the difference in how you present yourself to others and how you feel about yourself via their reactions.

Many of the above are born out of slavery and the historical traumatic experiences of Black people. Therefore, these same behaviors are passed down from one generation to the next and can be burdensome for both the giver and the receiver.

Feed Your Spirit, Focus Your Mind, and Train Your Body

I encourage you to do what you can to enhance your spirit, mind, and body. When they are healthy and thriving, you are at your best. You can start with feeding your spirit each day. One way to do this is by investigating your interests. Explore new ideas and concepts that interest you. Begin to live a life that allows you to feel free. Your spirit grows when you have the freedom to be yourself.

Second, focus your mind on the things that matter. When you know what matters in your life, make sure those are the things that get your attention. Don't waste your mental energy on things that are of little consequence or beyond your control. Allow yourself to focus on growing your abilities more and more each day. Learn to be in control of your thoughts and attention. Keep your mind focused on your goals.

Third, train your body. This is the only body you have, so greatly respect it. Take wonderful care of it and know that each day you are becoming stronger, healthier, and fitter.

Your body houses your spirit and your mind, so it is your temple. It's important to take care of your temple and train it consistently. Don't allow the negative energy of others to infiltrate your mind, body, or spirit. Cultivate a daily practice of mental, physical, and spiritual fitness. Make fitness in these three areas a priority.

Tell yourself each day, "Today, I am focused on my mind, spirit, and body. Everything else is on hold. I feed my spirit, focus my mind, and train my body." Make this your new mantra.

You can use these reflective questions to guide you daily.

Self-Reflection Questions:

1. How can I feed my spirit each day? How will this impact my life?
2. How well am I able to focus? What am I focusing on each day?
3. How would I rate my overall health and fitness? What can I do to strengthen my health?

Be the person who breaks the
cycle. If you were judged, choose
understanding. If you were
rejected, choose acceptance.
If you were shamed, choose
compassion. Be the person you
needed when you were hurting,
not the person who hurt you.
Vow to be better than what
broke you—to heal instead of
becoming bitter so you can act
from your heart, not your pain.

— Lori Deschene

CHAPTER 5

EXPLORE, UNLOCK, AND RELEASE

"Pride and power fall when the person falls, but discoveries of truth
form legacies that can be built upon for generations."
~Criss Jami, *Venus in Arms*

"Family pathology rolls from generation to generation like a fire in
the woods, taking down everything in its path, until one person in one
generation has the courage to turn and face the flames. That person
brings peace to his ancestors and spares the children that follow."
~Terry Real

This section of the book will help us to explore the many
ancestral and legacy burdens we discussed in the previous
section. It will allow us the opportunity to take a deeper
dive into those unfamiliar places of deep hurts, guilt, and shame.
Exploring is where we identify the parts of our lives that have been

hindering us from moving forward. We explore by being with and curious about ourselves.

Exploration is the beginning of acknowledging and accepting. When we explore, we give ourselves permission to be open to the possibilities of what lies ahead. We can explore, recognize where we fall short, and do nothing with what we find. That's okay. But it's not good enough. What good will come from just exploring and not being curious about what we find? What good could come from exploring and not allowing ourselves to move beyond the new knowledge? In this chapter, I encourage you to look beyond what you have found and to use the keys of curiosity to unlock the ancestral and legacy burdens you have been carrying all these years.

Ramona was one of the busiest marketing executives at work. Before and after her long workday shifts, she took care of her husband and kids. Any time she had left went to helping her parents and grandparents, raising her nieces and nephews, and helping others at her church who said they needed her.

Ramona was so busy she rarely had even a minute to rest before someone else needed help again. At times she was even too busy to pay attention to her own health. She didn't stop to take care of herself or to think about the stress and exhaustion. One day, Ramona got very sick and couldn't get out of bed. Though exhausted and ill, all she could think about was missing work, not being able to cook or clean or take care of her family, and not being available to her church members. Ramona was so sick that she spent more than two weeks in bed.

Because of her health, Ramona almost lost her job. Her kids ran wild throughout the house. Her husband tried to cook but failed. Her parents, grandparents, and others complained about her being sick. As she laid sick in bed, Ramona slowly realized she was so busy taking care of everyone else that she forgot to take care of herself. *I've focused so much on others, but I completely forgot about my own health*, she thought.

As Ramona's strength returned, she decided to gather her family, friends, coworkers, and church family to inform them that there would be big changes ahead. She wasn't going to neglect her health anymore. It was time for her to find a balance between helping them and taking care of herself. Now, they would have to help out too.

A few years ago, I found myself at a crossroads in my life. I, too, was like Ramona. I was working at least three different jobs and was spending little to no time with myself, family, or friends. It was all about work. I would hustle from one job to the next, sometimes not eating (or eating in my car) on the way to the next job. My friends would call and ask, "Are you home?" Before I could answer, they would say, "I bet you are not; you must be at your fifth job. How many jobs do you have now?" We would both laugh, and although it helped to pay my expenses, all that work was causing me a lot of stress.

It was not until one of my consulting jobs ended that I started to experience withdrawals and anxiety. I was forced to look at what was causing me to feel the way I did. As I began to explore, the truth became clearer. I had become a workaholic. I was suffering from workaholism. This may not seem serious, but it is.

Researchers have described workaholism as an excessive commitment to work that results in neglecting other important aspects of life. Work addiction can result from a need to control one's life, an overly competitive drive to succeed, being raised by a workaholic parent or role model, and low self-esteem or self-image. For me, I was addicted to working and for all the wrong reasons. It's what we in the addiction world call a process addiction. I would spend all my time hustling to get from one consulting job to the next. It was during these moments that I got my "high." I worked so that I wouldn't have to stop and feel or pay attention to what was going on in my life. I was emotionally numb. I was shut down. I had locked down every emotion possible and left them somewhere deep inside of me.

Workaholism is often easily accepted by society and, at times, even rewarded. We are encouraged to work hard, and when we do, it is seen as commendable. No one told me I was overdoing it. In fact, I was being supported, encouraged, and rewarded. I believed that if I worked longer hours, I was more productive. But I learned the hard way because I crashed and burned.

It wasn't until I gave myself permission to explore the underlying reasons for my workaholism that I learned to unlock the real reason behind my need to always work…to "get high" or not feel. Before I could make the next move, I had to bring it all to my conscious mind, then to the forefront, and begin to work on what was driving me to work, work, work. The more I explored, the more I learned about the underlying cause and root of my workaholism.

I remember during this time, especially the first few months in therapy, I was in denial about how much I was working and what it was doing to me. The more my therapist pushed, the more I would push back at her. One day, as I was pushing back, she said to me, "What are you afraid of finding out?" I looked at her, and I simply replied, "Nothing." But deep down inside, the question was haunting me. It was at that moment I knew I could not resist anymore. I had come too far to turn back now. And I kid you not, the day I left her office and got into my car to drive home, I turned on the CD player and heard this song: "Can't Give Up Now" by Mary, Mary.

Like I've said, music speaks to me. I sat there in my car with tears running down my cheeks. I couldn't turn back. I had gone too far. Nevertheless, I went on fighting.

You see, this thing called vulnerability showed up. My tears reflected my mixed emotions. I was angry because the therapist had broken through my "tough girl" exterior. You know, that shield I had created for such a long time that held me together—the one that made me look and feel confident, the never-let-them-see-you-sweat persona. And no one had ever done that before. I knew how to manage my emotions and how to stay calm during a storm, and here she was standing next to me (figuratively), behind the shield, without an invitation (well, I did invite her when I decided to see a therapist) and pushing me to search within myself for the answers I was not willing or ready to embrace. So yes, the tears were that of anger. After all, I was only there to do surface work.

After the anger faded, the tears were different, and appreciation slowly kicked in. Someone was willing to look beyond my "well-put-together" exterior and was challenging me to see my own vulnerability, reminding me of my humanness and that whatever was underneath or behind the shield was a part of me. I appreciated her not coddling or being intimidated by me. She empathetically confronted my crap and forced me to deal with it.

Yes, I cried because I finally felt seen, heard, and valued in a way I never had before. This was different, and I knew I couldn't go back to who I had created. Although I kept on fighting and pushing back with my stubbornness, I've learned that healing brings an awareness and a reality that says, "You can't go back or continue to keep doing the things that have kept you from living in the present." It forces you to shift the way you have been moving in the world from fear to acceptance and into action. I couldn't give up, and I needed to be *still*, which reminded me of the lyrics to the song "Still" by Brian Courtney Wilson.

Too often, as women, we spend too much time helping others without thinking about our own lives. We work all day, take care of our family, and help others because we care about them. Unfortunately, we sometimes let all this work exhaust us and make us sick. We don't stop to take care of our health or mental wellness, nor do we think about all the stress we create for ourselves daily. We become so focused on helping other people and our families that we lose ourselves in the process.

Admittedly, and ashamedly, it's easy to neglect your health while you work. It's easy to forget to take breaks or to schedule in self-care moments while you're raising kids or helping other family members. However, it's important to keep in mind that your life also matters! If you become sick or exhausted, then you won't be able to help anyone. You'll become a burden for others instead. So I invite you to strive to find a balance between taking care of others and taking care of yourself. Soon enough, others will learn to rely on you less; you'll have more time for yourself, and everyone will be better off!

In many Black families, like in many other families, there are expectations for women and expectations for men. However, in the Black community, those roles and expectations manifest differently because of our traumatic past. Let's look at women in the Black community.

The notion of the strong Black women trope has almost always been a part of the Black family. This is a myth. Now don't get me wrong—there's nothing wrong with being a strong Black woman. The challenges arise in how we view and see strength. This belief is grounded in history. The notion of the strong Black woman stereotype could be killing us. It's time for us as Black women to explore this concept deeper and unlock the ancestral beliefs we have been holding on to about what it means to be a strong Black woman.

As Black women, because of those who paved the way, we have now been given the opportunity to reach for the American Dream. We are gaining access to higher positions in Corporate America, the health-care system, and many other places. Yet we are still expected to abide by the traditional roles and obligations. We continue to be available and provide for the people who depend on us—our spouses, our children, our aging parents—all while maintaining our homes. We are carrying a load no one else is expected to carry, and we avoid turning to others for help until it's too late. It is vitally important to take care of yourself while taking care of others.

Many Black girls observe this behavior and then pass this same belief and behavior down to their offspring. Some mothers tell their daughters to stay with a man even though they are not happy, because this is what they did. This is an example of a burden that some Black women carry.

For the Black man this looks very different. Deeply rooted systemic issues are the cause of the many challenges faced by Black men. They are conditioned to believe that they are not supposed to seek help. They experience isolation and feelings of unworthiness and are often devalued. They are burdened with the belief that the only role they have is to provide for their families and to protect their children—a belief based on society's value of what you do and not who you are. And when they cannot or do not do this, they fall back on what they observed from the other men in their lives and the community (i.e., Maladaptive behaviors such as infidelity, substance use, intimate partner violence, and a host of other behaviors that have become burdensome to them and the people they are close to).

It is just as important for Black men to release their burdens and work toward healing. The releasing and the unburdening needs to happen so that he may can fulfill his destiny, contribute to his family and his community, and leave a legacy for the next generation of Black men.

Our ancestors have left us with many great legacies. But they also left legacies that continue to be burdensome. Unless we begin to take an inventory of why we behave and feel the way we do...why we continue to engage in behavior patterns that hurt us...and find ways to change those harmful patterns, we will continue to pass down those burdensome legacies to our children.

Fredrick Douglas once said, "It is easier to build strong children than to repair broken men." What I have learned in my work as a therapist is that many adults who show up in my office for emotional issues are often dealing with scars from their childhood and teenage years. It's time for us to release those burdens and let go of the baggage we are carrying—those of our ancestors and the ones we have picked up along the way.

Heal.
Heal, so that you don't ever have to
give a sarcastic tone to
uplifting messages.

Heal, so you never have to
make anyone else the object of
your frustration.

Heal, so that when someone tells
you they love you, you may,
allow yourself to believe them.

-Unknown

CHAPTER 6

RELEASING THE BURDEN

"Your beliefs become your thoughts, your thoughts become your words, your words become your actions, your actions become your habits, your habits become your values, your values become your destiny." ~Gandhi

"Even though you may want to move forward in your life, you may have one foot on the brakes. To be free, we must learn how to let go. Release the hurt. Release the fear. Refuse to entertain your old pain. The energy it takes to hang onto the past is holding you back from a new life. What is it you would let go of today?"
~Mary Manin Morrissey

Too many of us have been deafened by the voice of conformity, the voice of criticism, and the voice of condemnation. The side effects of this deafening include loneliness, shame, and anxiety. What I have learned is that trauma can stay with us long after a threat is gone. It can lodge itself into our felt experience and embed itself into our bodies and our minds. There's no greater battle than the battle between the parts of you that want to be healed and the parts of you that are comfortable and content in remaining broken.

This chapter discusses the importance of releasing the burdens that weigh us down. In the previous chapter, we focused on identifying the areas of our lives that have been burdensome. What does it mean to release? To release is to *let go*... Letting go of the things that no longer add value to your life and well-being. Letting go of the things in life that have been holding you back, holding you down, and keeping you chained and in bondage.

Here's a question: Have you ever tried holding your breath for a long time?

What does it feel like? I bet many of you would say it's uncomfortable. You might even say it feels like you're going to explode.

The breath you're holding can feel constricted and tight. In fact, the longer you hold it, the more dangerous it becomes. After a while, you can't hold it in any longer and are forced to release it. What happens when you release? What does it feel like?

I would imagine you feel a sense of relief once you start breathing again. So it is with emotional and psychological burdens we carry. They can become stifling, constricted, and trapped in our hearts, minds, bodies, and souls. But they don't have to stay there.

I have found that many of the burdens we carry are deeply connected to traumatic experiences many of us have personally or vicariously endured. Therefore, it is important that we first realize the prevalence of trauma in our own lives and the lives of those we come into contact with. This notion of realization is just that—a realization. It opens us to have compassion for ourselves and others. Second, we must recognize how trauma affects all individuals. Whether big or small, we all have been affected one way or another. However, recognition doesn't stop there. You must want to make an effort to release the burden of the traumas you're carrying, your own and that of your ancestors. Finally, we must learn to respond by putting knowledge in place. What does it mean to put knowledge in place? Well, simply put, it means to take action. Releasing requires action. To start the process of releasing burdens, we must be active participants in the process. A cleansing may need to happen—a detoxification of sorts.

I recently read a story about the Golden Buddha. The story speaks of the king of Thailand, who ordered his men to search through the ruins of ancient temples to bring some of them back to the city. So they did. They found an ordinary statue made of a common cheap, ancient plaster. Because no one noticed it, it was moved, never to be seen again.

Years later, a new temple was built. This temple was big enough to hold the statue, and as they were moving it, the ropes snapped, and the statue crashed and broke. But in reality, it was not broken: the plastic was a façade, and the statue was made of pure gold. The monks researched information about the statue and realized it had been created years ago, during the 13th century, where monks would sit in the shadow of the statue and meditate. Then in the 1700s, a foreign army invaded their villages, and the villagers were raped, sacked, and burned to the ground. The monks were scared; they protected the statue by covering it with plaster and shards of colored glass to make it look worthless and ordinary so that it would not be harmed. It worked because the statue remained unnoticed and unappreciated for years.

So it begs the question: How many people looked at the mud and plaster, not realizing it covered over five tons of solid gold?

As I kept reading, I came across a commentary that said, "We're all born a Golden Buddha. While we're in our infancy, we shine brilliantly and purely. We create things. We speak the truth. We dream. We give from our hearts. Until we feel threatened. Then we do what everyone else who came before us did, and we cover our true identity with plaster and mud—so that we won't be noticed, or hurt, or humiliated, or broken. Years pass, and we forget who we are. The world relates to us as plaster and mud, and we look in the mirror each day and believe that is all we are. Until a shock comes. We get dropped, or our plans and our dreams get shattered, and we're forced to do something remarkable. That's the moment when the mud and the plaster fall away, and we see ourselves for what we really are. This is the unburdening, and this is the release that needs to happen in order for us to heal."

Get this: there's hope.

I'd like to introduce what I call the P.A.U.S.E. Method. It's a method I developed when doing my own work during the releasing process.

P: Pay attention to what and where you feel it in your body. Where is it coming from? Whose voice are you hearing? What story are you telling yourself?

A: Accept and acknowledge it, and know that it's okay. Give yourself permission to feel and to be present in the moment. Remember, feelings are just feelings and nothing else. Experience it without shame, blame, or judgment.

U: Unlock the belief that is holding you hostage. Allow yourself to bring the belief into focus and unlock it by being curious.

S: Sit with the belief, and identify the feeling that comes with it. Once you have identified the feeling, locate where in your body you might be feeling it. Think about whether this belief is helping or hindering your growth and/or your healing. Be open and curious.

E: Embrace, engage, and evaluate your relationship to the thought or feeling. Ease into the discomfort and embrace it with gratitude and without judgment.

So many of us work hard to not feel the feelings. We either sleep it away, drink it away, smoke it away, eat it away, hide behind it, or run from it. If only we would sit with it, we will see that the pain doesn't last forever. To heal it, we must feel it and go through it. As James Fortune said in his song "There Ain't Nothing," it's the only way that we can be free.

Your anger?
It's telling you where you feel powerless.
Your anxiety?
It's telling you that something in your
life is off-balance.
Your fear?
It's telling you what you care about.
Your apathy?
It's telling you where you're
overextended and burnt out.
Your feelings aren't random,
they are messengers. And if you
want to get anywhere, you need
to be able to let them speak to
you, and tell you what you
really need.

Brianna Wiest

CHAPTER 7

RECLAIMING YOUR THOUGHTS, FEELINGS AND EMOTIONS

"This is our legacy. This is our chance to make a difference. Together, we will break the silence and break the cycle!"
~Taraji P. Henson

Never before have we in the Black community been more aware of our deficiencies than right now. Never before have we had the knowledge and the data, the sense of community, and the ability to break down barriers than we have right now. A heightened awareness of our situation extends beyond our homes and families and into the larger community. We have begun to educate ourselves on the fallacies of the past and have begun to understand the cruel form of living and the lack of self-love we have been punishing ourselves with. This is the opportunity generations of struggle, strife, self-hate, and emotional denial have led up to. Our chance to free ourselves from the invisible chains that continue to tie us down and restrict us from living more positively lies within our reach.

Why Should We Do It?

From the outside looking in, taking on the challenge of improving our mental health seems obvious. Why wouldn't we want to? But as explored in the last chapter and in earlier parts of this book, the idea of improving one's mental health does not always fit the profile of BIPOC, who in large swathes continue to view the mental health field as unnecessary, untrustworthy, or both. This mindset and the cultural belief that experiencing negative emotions and unpleasant memories is a sign of a weak person remain potent in our community.

The most important reason to pursue better mental health is to stop the emotional suicide that we are daily perpetrating against ourselves. It starts when we identify unwanted or unwelcome feelings and emotions in ourselves that do not cohabit well with our commonly held beliefs about who we are, our identifying characteristics, our self-perception, and how we want to be viewed by others. I know this way of being all too well.

We want to be seen by others as strong and fierce, confident and in control...self-reliant and independent, not needing handouts or assistance from anyone. If our childhood was bad, we wear the experiences from it like a badge of honor, and pay it forward to our own children. While we might secretly want to replace the harsh words and cruel punishments with kinder, softer responses, we are stuck in a repetitive cycle of the generations who have come before us. That's the way it's always been done. That's the way we learned it. That's the way we will carry it forward.

When present-day situations—be they the actions of others, our own memories welling up, a tone of voice, a smell, or even a taste—bring up trauma from our pasts, we kill those feelings and emotions as swiftly as you might yank the plug out of the wall if a kitchen appliance started throwing sparks and sputtering. It might feel like you've solved the problem by suppressing how you feel, because the feelings are gone for now, just like the sparks die down when there is a lack of electricity flowing into the appliance. But just like the blender is still broken, you are still broken.

Once we cut off those emotions, we try to bury them as deep as possible. We pile our busy lives on top of them. We throw ourselves into our work. We throw ourselves into our families. We lock into our churches and volunteer to occupy any free time that would otherwise lead to the welling up of those unpleasant thoughts. We take on a second job or a side hustle. Sometimes, we bury our emotions in less savory ways. We begin or rekindle destructive, negative behaviors that allow us to mute those emotions we find unpleasant or unsettling.

Common substance abuse problems in the African American US population are illicit drug use (13.7% have used in the past month) and marijuana use (12.2% have used in the past month)—both higher than the general US population (Kaliszewski 2020). Addictions run deeper than illegal substance abuse, of course. Drinking, smoking, vaping, sexual addictions, *food addictions*, violence, crime, and other detrimental behaviors can all be ramped up in an attempt to negate unwanted emotions. Of course, burying emotions doesn't make them disappear. It only allows them to fester more and more until they reach a point where they can no longer be contained; they then bubble up to the surface to do even more unpredictable damage.

When people recall those traumatic experiences, they reactivate responses based on the original impact. Tamping down past traumas makes us less aware of ourselves and our traumas, which makes it extremely difficult, if not impossible, to handle them correctly and appropriately. We also perpetuate a state of denial that becomes so frequent we come to accept it as our reality. We have convinced ourselves that if we do not think about these traumas or accept them as the truth, they will cease to exist. The longer we go without an incident of trauma, the more convinced we are that we have defeated these past incidents.

Being in denial does not merely affect our ability to separate fact from fiction. It can have lasting physical effects on us as well. It alters our mood, makes us more prone to depression, and negatively affects our cardiovascular health, including putting us at more risk for hypertension and stroke. Just as the traumas of our parents and our more distant relatives have come to us, so too will we transmit intergenerational and transgenerational trauma and burdens because the lack of mental health care extends beyond us *if we do not address it.*

Transgenerational trauma refers to historical trauma and burdens that have become parts of Black culture—whether we are willing to admit and accept them or not. While slavery is the most well-known and prevalent part of that burden, it is not the only one, and for many BIPOC it is not even the most damaging. Discrimination and racism are equally powerful traumas that have plagued Blacks for more than a century. As often as we continue to face them in our own modern society, we must be aware that at least some of this burden comes from the inherited trauma and responses our ancestors have passed on to us as well.

As we know from our shared history, racism and discrimination did not end the day Abraham Lincoln freed the slaves in the 1860s. If anything, these practices grew far worse in many areas of the country, particularly in the South during the following period of Reconstruction. Whites who had previously owned Black slaves not only lost their 'property' and workforce but were now being told they had to treat Blacks as equals in all things, from voting to education, to being members of the workforce. Many states rebelled against this notion and passed laws that separated Blacks from Whites in all things, and severely punished Blacks who broke the laws and attempted to use facilities designated as Whites only—a practice that continued for close to 100 years.

As a result, from generation to generation, many Blacks carried the notion that they were inferior to Whites, that Whites were naturally prejudiced against them, and that crossing or angering a White person would be tantamount to harsh punishment. This led to many forms of trauma being passed down among Blacks, with notions like keeping your head down, never complaining, never making eye contact, and 'keep stepping' becoming rooted in our subconscious makeup. These historical blights have kept Blacks from realizing their full potential, being comfortable in their own skin, making quicker progress in integrating into the general society, and advancing in education, political, and industrial capacities.

Our intergenerational trauma and burdens do not go as far back in history but are just as potent and debilitating, depending on how deep the trauma runs and how it is triggered in the current generation. The same addictions we spoke of in the previous section rear their ugly heads as intergenerational trauma. If we grew up watching our parents or other caretakers drink, smoke, or abuse drugs, the likelihood that we will fall victim to the same vices increases dramatically, even if we associate our parents' addictions with unhappiness and sickness, and as the cause of their deaths.

Furthermore, if domestic violence or abuse was prevalent in our parents' homes during their formative years, our parents are much more likely to carry on those harmful habits to us, their own children, and we are much more likely to do the same. People in successive generations tell themselves that what's happening is just the way of the world and the way things are done in the family, never questioning why the harmful habits are never talked about, confronted, or handled differently. If our families have a history of alcoholism, drug abuse, unemployment, incarceration, abandonment, infidelity, or anything else that disrupts family life and causes undue stress, the chances of those issues being passed on to subsequent generations is higher than for those whose ancestors did not deal with them.

How Do We Do It?

If we break through the struggle and strife that comes up as we work to improve our mental health by reclaiming our thoughts, emotions, and feelings, we make significant progress; we are that much closer to experiencing healing. Still, it is not as easy as making the decision. We must commit to adopting a new way of thinking—both internally and externally—and doing a significant amount of work in uncharted territories toward the purpose of self-discovery, self-acceptance, and self-love.

Each of these ways we relate to ourselves is important and needs our attention. But trying to address all of them at once can be overwhelming and cause people to shut down as their ingrained misconceptions about who they are and what they are worth threaten to destabilize their progress and push back against their strides. Improving in these areas is often done only with the help of a therapist or counselor.

Many BIPOC fear sharing the journey of self-healing they are attempting, even with their own close-knit circle of family and friends, because they do not want to be the subject of ridicule or mockery for trying to break free from the norm and establish something better for themselves. Because of the cultural bias that remains firmly entrenched against this form of discovery, great care must be taken when attempting such a feat, to avoid negative reactions that can cause people to feel they are out of their element, betraying their family or acting atypical of their heritage.

The process is not so much one of steps on a path; the aim is for us to become more aware than we previously were, and to use that awareness to enjoy a richer, fuller life experience. It should be noted that doing the work to heal does not guarantee a lifetime of happiness. Having good mental health and always being happy and joyful are not constant bedfellows. Mental health refers to the ability to interpret, understand, process, and properly respond to all of the thoughts, feelings, and emotions we encounter over a lifetime. Outside of God Himself, no one can predict our level of happiness and contentment throughout the rest of our days.

The experiences necessary to evolve into a more stable individual with improved mental health include:

- **Overcoming personal and communal denial:** We must move past our dismissal of things we pretend do not matter, did not happen, or do not affect us. We must do this individually and, more importantly, as a community. That doesn't mean you need to convince everyone in your neighborhood that they are still facing traumas of slavery, racism, discrimination, violence, and abuse that their forefathers encountered. It does mean accepting that these things have caused us to feel beat down, hopeless, defeated, powerless, and incapable of overcoming. We do not seek to deny that these events happened, only to deny that they are allowed to continue having power over us. For us to control our own thoughts in the present and prepare for a more stable future, we must conquer the specter of the past.

- **Resisting the emotional and physical responses of trauma:** The power of trauma runs deep in our subconscious. A certain smell that reminds you of your childhood home where one of your parents physically abused you can make your heartbeat accelerate and activate your fight-or-flight mechanism, even if you're sitting on a couch or riding in an elevator. Hearing a certain term or phrase someone always used to say before punishing you with a belt can make you sweat and revert to the mentality of a five-year-old even though you're ten times that age. To combat the responses we have from buried trauma, or transgenerational/intergenerational trauma, we must be able to recognize it in all forms. Calling something by its name and recognizing it in the moment are the surest ways to strip away its power. Being able to recognize that past trauma cannot harm us in our current life if we do not let it happen is a major step toward having stable mental health.

- **Self-love:** This is perhaps the most vital quality and the most difficult to attain when you are starting this healing process as an adult. It does not mean we view ourselves as perfect or even better than most. It does mean that we accept ourselves just the way we are and love ourselves for it, through any and all perceived flaws, mistakes, and deficiencies. It is the very essence of looking into the mirror and smiling at the person looking back at you—seeing their strengths and successes, not their weaknesses and failures.

- **Becoming more aware of the connection between your body and mind and learning to control your physical and mental states:** For many people, when they experience fear, stress, anger, or disappointment, those negative emotions often manifest themselves as physical maladies. Many people are never able to appreciate the connection, and they allow their emotions to consume not only their mental health but their physical well-being as well. The connection is specific and verified. Our minds have a significant influence over our bodies that is undeniable and *undeniably* powerful. To master one, we must master both and understand that letting our negative emotions consume our current mind frame also affects our bodies. Taking appropriate time to properly process your emotions is a necessary component to keep from losing sight of these aspects of your life.

- **Experiencing all of our emotions:** Opening ourselves up to feelings such as grief and sadness or fear and doubt may seem counterintuitive to the idea of becoming more mentally healthy, but it is essential to growth. Embracing happiness and joy, and confidence and success is easy. Those emotions don't leave lingering negative effects, nor do they sneak up on us later to send us spiraling down again. The so-called negative emotions are felt when we are seeking protection from the possibility of future events. We get scared when we fear we might lose a job. We get angry when we believe a best friend has talked about us behind our backs. The hallmark of good mental health is to embrace these emotions, let them wash over us, break them down to expose their roots, and then move past them in a healthy matter by determining how they are affecting us, how we can accept them, and how to process them so that they are managed completely, not hidden away.

- **Increasing self-awareness:** What is causing the feelings we experience so potently? What in our own makeup causes them to exert such powerful effects on us? What in our past causes a particular set of circumstances to resonate negatively, positively, or powerfully within us, more so than within our circle of peers? Exploring inwardly is the way to solve this conundrum. It is getting down to the essence of who we are, how we arrived here, and what our mindset looks like.

- **Embracing all parts of yourself, including the shadows:** This discipline is a close cousin to self-love. We gain strength by accepting all parts of ourselves—"warts and all," as the old saying goes. Many of us have many areas of darkness, places we try to avoid and that we desperately want to keep secret from those around us. But even the darkness of abuse, addiction, violence, and so forth, part of who we are remains. The head does not deny the existence of the hand because it is withered and old or missing a finger. It embraces it and continues to work with it for the brightest future possible.

- **Understanding nonverbal communication:** Our tone of voice, our posture, the way we square our shoulders, the way we set our jaw…all of it combines to create the way we speak to others and influences how they perceive us. Through these nonverbal forms of communication, we often give off a sense of hostility, aggressiveness, bitterness, or other emotions that can show our wariness to situations or cause others to be wary of us. We imitate those around us when we adapt these forms of communication, and more often than not they are happening subconsciously to the point that we are not even aware of them until they are specifically pointed out to us. Learning to model positive and inviting facial gestures, posture, and other forms of communication is vital to us being successful at communicating our wants and needs to others in the future.

- **Leading with empathy and compassion:** We don't use these two-character traits nearly enough. We often resort to the mentality of "taking care of me and mine" and don't worry about how the rest of the world is taken care of. In doing so, we harden our hearts against the spirit of community, brotherhood, and other commonalities we feel we are often denied of due to our past trauma of prejudice and racism. Instead of pushing these things to the side, however, in our new frame of mental health, we can lead with them, setting the tone in conversations and engagements to show others that we care about them, care for their thoughts and wishes, and wish to help them as they help us form a stronger community together.

- **Self-care:** It goes hand in hand with self-love. When we believe in that reflection in the mirror, we are far more apt to want to stay healthy and happy. Self-care seems simple on the surface but can be far more difficult to maintain when we let negative emotions regularly consume us. It involves getting enough sleep, eating healthy, minimizing distractions and addictions, and taking time for *we* as a people, a practice that is often looked down upon in the BIPOC community. Keeping track of our thoughts and feelings can be done via writing and journaling, which serves the dual purpose of giving us that vital "me" time and keeping us honest and transparent when it comes to our thoughts and feelings, so that what's negative is consistently brought to the light for examination.

Working through each layer
of the self is the key to inner
healing.

— VEX KING

Chapter 8

Healing the Wounds

"It's always hard to deal with injuries mentally, but I like to think about it as a new beginning. I can't change what happened, so the focus needs to go toward healing and coming back stronger than before." ~Carli Lloyd

Stopping intergenerational and transgenerational trauma is not an individual journey, but a collective dream for Blacks to break the cycle of allowing the past to influence their presents and futures. Because of the rich heritage that Blacks share—one that sprawls across influences from Mother Africa, the Caribbean, Europe, and beyond—there are elements of traditional trauma healing and rehabilitation that work effectively for some, while others get more benefit from therapists who tap deeper into Black cultural roots, using elements of culture, faith, symbolism, dance, cooking, and other Afrocentric healing practices. In this chapter, we will discuss these various practices and how they can be used to break the cycle of generational trauma once and for all.

Healing of Personal Traumas

Personal trauma is the easiest type to recognize but often the most difficult to get past. We have directly been affected by the trauma, be it a divorce, an illness, job loss, income loss, a miscarriage, death of a pet, home loss, or anything else that is front and center. The emotional trauma that results often leaves us feeling numb, disconnected, or mistrustful of others. As stated in previous chapters, many Blacks make the tragic mistake of trying to either bury the trauma deep down in their minds or pretend that it does not bother them, and that it's just "part of life." Healing from this type of trauma involves opening oneself up to accept help and healing, two things that are not naturally a part of many BIPOC's lives. Here are the steps toward healing this type of trauma using the traditional method:

1. **Be willing to heal.** Don't assume there's something wrong with you or that you are broken. Trauma happens to every single person who has ever lived on this planet. Letting yourself accept that you can and should want to feel better is a big first step.

2. **Accept the support of your loved ones.** Being the "strong as iron" person in the family only lasts so long before that façade shatters. You've heard the phrase that it takes a village to raise a child; well, it also takes a village to heal a friend. Weed out toxic people in your life and share your attempts to recover from trauma only with those who love, respect, and support you through thick and thin.

3. **Get professional help.** A big linchpin for Blacks is admitting that a psychologist or counselor can help them make progress. If you distrust a particular idea, work to find the

right professional to help you as you would buying a new car or going on a first date; be picky and only move forward with someone you feel comfortable with.

4. **Mindfulness and meditation.** M&M makes it easy to remember, right? Meditation lets you control the thoughts racing around in your mind and is a tremendous way to start your day off right, reminding yourself of the good things in your life instead of letting bad thoughts creep in. Mindfulness is vital to making sure you don't let yourself slip during the day to the point of that old trauma rising to impact your life and negatively affect your actions and thoughts during the day.

5. **Get moving.** Even if exercise is not on your daily agenda, it's time to flip the script. Why? Because exercise generates endorphins in your brain, and those are going to create positive feelings throughout your body, not to mention enhance your sense of stability and safety.

Healing of Collective Traumas

Collective traumas are those that damage an entire community. They can look very different for different populations. For instance, a fire that tears through an apartment building... A school shooting... The COVID-19 pandemic... Racial tension that spills over into violence and riots. They all qualify. They often make people feel powerless and beat down. In Black communities, it happens so frequently that it often simply becomes a way of life.

Healing from collective trauma is best done by having those who were impacted by it create some sort of positive shared meaning around it. A nationally traumatic event like the terrorist attacks of September 11, 2001, is a good example of this. Memorials were created for the victims of the cowardly airplane hijackings—places where people could visit, reflect on those who had died, and share the bond of remembering with others in a public space. Establishing programs to help others who have experienced similar traumas or bringing grief counselors into the community to teach people tactics and techniques to release the trauma in healthy, positive ways are other ideas that nurture good intentions and let people heal at their own pace.

Exploring and Embracing the Positive Legacies of Your Ancestors

For many Blacks whose family history stretches back into the 19th century, it is no surprise to find out they have ancestors who were slaves; there were as many as four million at one point in the Southern United States. But Blacks should not be defined by the worst period of their race, no more than anyone else. Slavery, as well as the Jim Crow and Reconstruction eras that followed it, were bleak times in the lives of all Americans. But defining ourselves only by this point is diminishing the lives of all our ancestors who followed the Slavery era.

Many questions can be asked. What were our great-grandparents like? Were they part of the Great Migration of slaves leaving the South for a better life? Is that not something to be proud of? What about Blacks who realized that the South was not the place to be and dared to dream of a better life? Who were our first ancestors to become literate? To hold a job in management? To become an officer in the Armed Forces? To buy their own home? To start their own business? To graduate from college?

Every family's ancestors have stories, and while some of them might be wrought with the fear and oppression of slavery and its long-looming shadow, we cannot let it define everything about who we are. Using family records or some of the marvelous online research websites can find out who your ancestors really were and where they lived, what they accomplished, and what they believed in. Embrace these accomplishments and let the pride of them flow through you.

Unburdening the Legacy Wounds

When many people hear the word "legacy," they envision what a wealthy person leaves behind in his or her will—stocks and bonds, vacation homes, luxury automobiles, and money. But legacies for many Black people don't involve things we want, but rather things that sit heavy on our hearts and minds: a legacy of divorce, violence, drug abuse, unemployment, and/or broken families. It is ugly and messy and complicated. We often very much love the people behind these legacies, even as we despise what they have left on our doorstep that has shaped our early lives.

Legacy wounds are those that come to us because of what those before us have done. If our father and grandfather both served time in the state penitentiary, then we feel, unjustly so, that we or our children might be destined for the same fate. If our mother, both her sisters, and her grandmother all suffered from alcoholism that caused them to die at young ages and have multiple short-lived marriages, we may swear off relationships to avoid the same fate, and our view of alcohol might swing erratically from "I'll never touch a drop" to "It's in my blood, why deny it." It is one of the most difficult mental and psycho-logical barriers for Blacks to overcome—taking the perceived failures and shortcomings of our predecessors and making them into our own predestined outcomes. It creates a cultural blind spot. Most never even realize they have adopted their ancestor's thoughts and attitudes or acted out their faulty beliefs because of these wounds, but the blind spot is there all the same.

The question is why. Why do the actions of our ancestors, who lived their lives before we were even born, have such a powerful effect on us? The answer is obvious—it's because we are imprinted with these ideas and memories at an early age, and they carry forward, shaping us as we go along. But just because they are our earliest, foundational thoughts does not mean they have to endure. Decoupling who we are from the people who came before us is essential to finding mental and spiritual peace.

Variations of Healing Practices Available to People of Color

Every race has different practices and cultural implementations that it uses for various forms of healing—whether that be spiritual, emotional, or physical. For older cultures, some of these practices date back thousands of years and have origins based in mysticism, culinary skills, dance and song, and the power of myth. Many Black people have entirely different belief systems from each other, based on what part of the country they grew up in, what their religious beliefs are, and what sort of home environment they had. Whether a therapist or counselor suggests alternative healing practices or you, the individual seeking better mental health and freedom from inter-generational or transgenerational trauma, want to try a non-traditional technique, there are no wrong answers.

Consider these choices like items at a buffet. Some will look appealing to you; some will seem ridiculous. Keep an open mind and try the ones that resonate with you; it is likely that there is something already within you that is connecting you to this form of therapy. Unless you have an intense negative reaction to the activity, give it a try for two or three sessions to see how it works and how you feel afterward. If it's not a fit, try something else. Putting forth the effort is just as important as finding a technique that works. It is a symbol that you are prepared to move forward past the trauma and have adopted the mind frame that there is a better life out there for you.

The following are ideas for both therapists and individuals on alternative forms of healing practices that can play a beneficial role in breaking the cycle of intergenerational and transgenerational trauma.

- **Using cultural symbols and artifacts, or incorporating faith practices**

Too often we think of the era of slavery and the period after it only as a time when Blacks were beaten down, enslaved, lynched, imprisoned, and discriminated against. All of those things happened, but they weren't the all-encompassing description of Black culture. Our ancestors also made music and art, were inventors, and were proud, strong men and women who overcame long odds and obstacles to build a life, find a home, and raise their children the best way they knew how, under God's laws. This can be seen in the artifacts that survive those times: handmade clothing and toys and farming tools, belt buckles from Black soldiers who fought in the Civil War, decorations from the first Black churches that sprang up during Reconstruction, and symbols that predate the United States itself that came from Africa—masks, costumes, weapons, and artwork. It all was handcrafted by Blacks and breathed into life, and centuries later continue to showcase their innovation, their artistic creativity, their exquisite attention to detail, and their passion for crafting beautiful things. It is a wonderful lesson in what beautiful contributions Blacks have made to the world, even in the bleakest of conditions.

- **Using metaphors that operated across cultures to bridge the linguistic and cultural gap**

Storytelling is the great cultural equalizer. No matter your intelligence level, your education level, where you live, or how old you are, as long as you have eyes and ears, you can learn from it. Our most ancient relatives in tribes across the ocean passed on mythology, great events, and tales of conflict and of family through stories that resonated with anyone who heard them. Connecting Blacks to modern times and away from the trauma of the past can be difficult because they focus on what they know and what's always been done. Breaking free of the old ways might seem like an anathema to some, who see it as a betrayal of the color of their skin and the culture they hail from. Using metaphors that illustrate how change can make something better can help bridge the gap, such as the common childhood story of the caterpillar entering the cocoon and emerging as a butterfly.

- **Using cooking metaphors to portray concepts and skills**

The practice of cooking is a cornerpiece in Black culture. The vision of massive family gatherings or the whole neighborhood turning out for a big Sunday meal after church or a barbecue at the park or a celebration that doesn't even need a reason—with everyone pitching in and bringing enough dishes to feed an army—is one that is easily captured and brings warm feelings to the heart. We are so readily and eagerly available to pitch in for our community, but so unwilling to help ourselves when we face struggles. Using cooking metaphors is a fantastic way to connect with people who are unwilling or unable to see the truth that is right in front of them and to explain themes like needing assistance for a really big meal. Much as one does to solve a big problem—like releasing generational trauma—being able to be flexible in a recipe and doing likewise in how we choose to live our lives differently than those who came before us (even trying new recipes that might surprise us) can be locked into trying new therapy techniques as a way to improve our mental health.

- **Use of cultural metaphors to convey concepts and understanding of family boundaries**

The family dynamic changes every generation, sometimes imperceptibly, sometimes by great leaps and bounds. Understanding how families are adapting to the new culture of being Black in America is important for therapists to acknowledge before treatment begins. Blacks are more likely to become single parents and also to live in extended-family households than Whites are, which can lead to very different familial roles and viewpoints about things like marriage and commitment. Appropriate family boundaries can get skewed in these types of environments: privacy is reduced to a bare minimum, adults make decisions for the approval of their parents rather than what's best for themselves, and children are often thrust into adult roles that they are too physically and emotionally immature to handle (i.e., taking care of younger children for long stretches of time). Using cultural metaphors can help individuals understand what life should look like as compared with what life does look like in their own environment or the one they grew up in, without the individuals feeling threatened.

- **Identify and validate the actual (tangible), symbolic (intangible), and secondary (i.e., anniversaries) losses**

Just like there are many different types of traumas, there are different types of losses. While they typically elicit different reactions and associated grief, they are all valid and need to be recognized by both counselor and patient as real and dealt with in a healthy, safe manner. Actual (tangible) losses are the events that happen to us and cause us grief: the death of a loved one or a close friend. Secondary losses are those things that happen as a result of the actual losses. For example, the death of a loved one alters other relationships, can cause financial strife, or might result in someone having to change schools or relocate to a new home, city, or state. Secondary losses also involve the extended grief of anniversaries of the day of the original trauma, such as the day of someone's death, the day a person found out his or her spouse had been unfaithful, or the anniversary of a divorce. Symbolic or intangible losses go even deeper. They surmise what a person meant to you, what their role was in society, the support they gave you, the knowledge that you could always get great advice from them, etc. They are intangible because person may not even be aware of them. When many people lose a parent, part of the grief they feel is that the sense of coming home is gone. Even if their parents no longer live in their original house, many people feel that nothing can be truly bad if they still have their parents to go to, lean on for support, etc. Parents might not know their children feel that way, but it is a type of trauma that exists beneath the surface and might not even be recognizable by the person suffering from it for some time.

Complimentary Afrocentric Healing Practices

A powerful way to break free of the negative connotations many Blacks experience due to generational trauma is to celebrate Afrocentrism through healing practices that either derive from African cultures or have been adapted from other Black communities, such as the Caribbean countries. Many of these practices are commonplace in multiple cultures, but adapting and exploring them with an Afrocentric slant will often help people connect to the positives of their heritage and help them break the cycle of trauma and negative thinking. Such practices include:

- **Yoga/Meditation (including breathing exercises)**

While traditional yoga is typically done quietly and individually, some Afrocentric practices are more embracing of the group environment and sharing the power and freedom of movement with others. Typical poses of hands lifted, stretching toward the sky, and embracing being free focus on the practice of being able to make your own decisions and life choices.

- **Drumming**

This ancient approach uses rhythm to promote health and self-expression. The Minianka healers of West Africa were using therapeutic rhythm techniques thousands of years ago for physical, mental, and spiritual health. Scientific studies show that it can lower blood pressure, reduce stress, and create a period of deep relaxation. It also produces feelings of insight, understanding, and truth by synchronizing the frontal and lower areas of the brain.

- **Dance/Dance Movement Therapy (DMT)**

DMT interventions can promote cultural relevance and community ownership, along with giving Blacks the environment to release emotions of all types through the movement of dance. Though research remains limited, it is gaining acceptance as an effective intervention to help Blacks heal from trauma. It can diminish symptoms of stress, depression, PTSD, and anger and also reduce stigma and help with reintegration into the community or family unit. It has been used as a trauma recovery technique dating back in history to the time of slavery.

- **Tapping/Emotional Freedom Technique (EFT)**

This alternative form of acupuncture uses the fingertips to stimulate energy points in the body. The power of positive energy has long been a tradition of African medicine. It works by tapping on acupressure meridians to release energy blockages. It is a great way to clear out feelings, which, in turn, can lead to limiting beliefs being eradicated.

- **Reiki (energy healing)**

Although Reiki got its start in Japan in the late 1800s, it also falls in line with the Afrocentric belief of the flow of energy through the body. It involves the transfer of energy—positive and negative—by laying of hands on one person by another. While the actual transfer might only be symbolic, the effect of concentrating on the desire to release or gain energy cannot be denied by those who practice it and reveal they feel that this practice reduces their pain, stress, and negative emotions. Some hospitals in the United States and Europe offer it as a form of therapy.

- **Nutrition**

It's amazing how adopting a healthier diet can positively affect how you feel and how much energy you have. The African heritage diet is a way of eating based on the healthy food traditions of people with African roots that focuses on colorful fruits and vegetables, tubers, beans, nuts, rice, and whole grains in abundance. Foods eaten a few times a week include homemade sauces, healthy oils, fish, eggs, poultry, and yogurt, while meats and sweets are saved for special occasions.

- **Massage**

Although not all that well-known, in most countries, there are multiple techniques of African massage that can go a long way toward releasing negative emotions from the body. The Congo massage begins with a long session of feet reflexology with baobab oil from the palaver tree, which is used by elders to tell stories to young people. The Rungu massage from Kenya uses wooden sticks to work on muscle tension. The Bamiléké massage from Cameroon uses sacred red earth known for its cleansing properties that is rolled into the muscles to deeply loosen them.

- **Writing/Journaling**

The power of writing should be obvious to any Black person who knows their literature. The likes of Toni Morrison, James Baldwin, Maya Angelou, and Langston Hughes have done more to show the heart, strength, soul, and suffering of Blacks than almost anyone thanks to their powerful prose and ability to be emotionally transparent. That practice is not just for selling books, either. When you write on the subjects you know best and on the ones that have deep-seated emotional power of *you*, you unlock hidden parts of your heart, soul, and mind, and allow yourself to work through these potent emotions one by one, bringing them to the surface, analyzing them, and beginning to find appropriate spaces inside yourself for them.

- **Herbalism/Plant Medicine**

Herbalism in Africa has been practiced for thousands of years, dating back to at least 1,500 BCE in Egypt. African herbs can be brewed, steamed, used as succulents, made into oil, cooked into food, and inhaled in the right environment. Some examples of African herbs to implement in this format are:

- Sceletium: A succulent used to aid in relaxation.
- Sutherlandia: A bush plant used for stress relief and to increase your appetite.
- Mucuna: A legume (bean) that can increase the release of dopamine, which increases feelings of happiness and maximizes your stress relief.

A person with ubuntu is open and available to others, affirming of others, does not feel threatened that others are able and good, for he or she has a proper self-assurance that comes from knowing that he or she belongs in a greater whole and is diminished when others are humiliated or diminished, when others are tortured or oppressed.

Desmond Tutu

CHAPTER 9

"ME" TO "WE," OUR COLLECTIVE HEALING

"The individual is the collective; the collective is the individual."
~Abhijit Naskar, Lives to Serve Before I Sleep

"Let's start working towards wellness, a healing in our community, a healing in relationships, so male and female can finally sit down and understand that, that young boy or young girl saw behavior exhibited by their parents that was negative and abusive, and they're going to pass it on." ~ Pam Grier, Author

"The act of claiming an identity can be transformational. It can provide healing and empowerment. It can weld solidarity within a community. And, perhaps most importantly, it can diminish power from an oppressor, a dominant group." ~ Simon Tam, Author

"I've been a therapist for more than forty years and certainly there is a place for "wise elders" in the healing process. But most people, most of the time, can heal themselves and those they love, with the help of their family, friends, and community." ~Jed Diamond, Author

I n 2014, I had the opportunity to travel to Africa—Botswana, to be exact. It was my first trip ever to an African country, and I was excited. The purpose of the trip was to learn about the country's success in fighting against the HIV/AIDS epidemic that was the cause of many deaths. I spent three weeks learning about this infectious disease that was taking the country by storm, especially the women and children. However, what impressed me the most was the country's approach to tackling this problem.

In 2013, Botswana had a population of two million people and, of that number, they had a 17.6% HIV prevalence rate, with an incidence rate estimated at 29% of new infections. At that time, males and females ages 30 to 34 were highly *affected*, while males and females ages 25 to 29 were highly *infected*. The primary mode of infection was heterosexual intercourse. During this time, HIV was the most important public health and medical problem and the leading cause of hospital admissions and deaths. It was considered to be the chief contributor to the orphan status in the country.

The first case of HIV was reported in 1985, and the government's response was reassurance instead of strategies to prevent new infections. In 1987, the country created a short-term plan that was basically screening and disposable needles. Between 1989 and 1993, they implemented a medium-term plan, where they focused on health issues and expanded their educational approach and their ABC approach: **A**bsenteeism, **B**e Faithful, **C**ondomize.

Many of these efforts did not change the outcome of the number of deaths they were seeing on a weekly basis, and during the late 1990s the country declared HIV/AIDS as a national emergency. They determined that the HIV response required a multisectoral approach involving major stakeholders. And with that, they established a new administrative structure.

From 2003 to 2009, they developed the National Strategic Framework for HIV/AIDS (NSF). The NSF goal was to address the many weaknesses evident in the national response such as:

- Lack of focused and coordinated implementation
- Weak management
- Inadequate legislature and policy
- Insufficient strategic guidance

To ensure that cross-cutting issues were identified, they outlined six critical themes: poverty, men, women, people living with HIV/AIDS (PLWHA), alcohol, and children/youth. The NSF then came up with five goals:

- Prevention
- Provision of care and support
- Strengthened management of national response
- Psychosocial and economic impact
- Provision of a strengthened legal and ethical environment

With those efforts, between 2010 and 2016, the NSF created a new vision for Botswana based on evidence and extensive consultation with stakeholders. They established fundamental principles and identified clear priorities in areas on prevention. The areas identified were:

- Preventing new infections
- Capacitating the national response
- Managing strategic information

- Maintaining integral commitments

With these priorities identified, the country included every stakeholder (finance, education, elderly, Ministry of Health, religious organizations, traditional healers, adolescents) possible to help combat the HIV/AIDS crisis. They received funding from many other countries and used the funding to prevent, intervene, and treat those infected with the virus. Their motto was "you may not be infected, but you are affected."

Botswana also instituted the Public Health Act. There were four items included in this act, and although this would not sit well in America, these four items helped to reduce the number of infections in the country. Here are the four items:

- Any medical facility could test patients for HIV without their knowledge or consent
- Doctors could disclose the status of an HIV patient to anyone the person has had sexual contact with
- In order to go through surgery or tooth extraction, you must be tested for HIV
- It is the duty of the infected individual to disclose their HIV status to whomever he or she has had sexual contact with

Additionally, Botswana brought together traditional healers and trained medical doctors to work together due to the belief that 80% of the citizens consult a traditional health practitioner either before or after visiting a public health facility. Therefore, they saw the benefit of having them come together to help combat the HIV/AIDS epidemic. This joining together was instrumental in saving the country. They believed that leadership and traditional medicine were inseparable. The goal of their intervention was to establish a viable, strong, healthy health care system in the country.

It was from this experience of traveling to Botswana I learned the value of collective care. What I learned specifically from that experience is what led me to the development of my collective care model. The model is based on the African concept of UBUNTU, which means, "I am because we are." The model starts with the individual and ends with the collective. It is continuous. It starts with self-awareness/discovery and collective awareness/discovery, then moves to self-preservation and collective preservation, and finally to self-liberation and collective liberation. If we are healed individually, we can be healed collectively. Let's walk through each section. At the end of this chapter, you will see a diagram of the model.

In summary, the purpose of the model is to focus on how we can take care of ourselves and our community as well. It is centered around the culture of Black communities, borrowing from our African ancestors of the community.

The model is based on the principles of caring for self and extending that care to the collective, such as in the African diaspora, where we believe in the power of the village. We also pay attention to the fact that if one person is doing well, then his or her family and community are doing well too. So I start with self-awareness to collective awareness, self-preservation to collective preservation, and self-liberation to collective liberation.

Self-Awareness: Coming into awareness of what one needs in order to be whole in mind, body, and spirit.

Collective Awareness: Coming into awareness of what the family/community needs.

Self-Preservation: Once you are aware of what you need, you can begin to take action and put into place the things you need to build up your reserves and replenish when needed.

Collective Preservation: Same as Self, but as a collective.

Self-Liberation: Awareness and preservation have to happen before one can be liberated. Therefore, liberation comes when you are finally able to be yourself—a sense of freedom without harm to others because you have given and continue to give to yourself so that you can give to others.

Collective Liberation: Same as above, but now your entire family/community is liberated as well, because they too have come together from a place of self-liberation, where they have extended that to each other as a community. So now you have a community of people who are free to give to each other in a way that is authentic, safe, healthy, and healing.

Self-Awareness

Self-awareness is the ability to know one's worth and remove the doubt of who one is. Therefore, self-awareness is the ability to discover one's true self, that is, to know how to discover one's strengths and weaknesses—the good, the bad, and also the limit.

Self-awareness cuts across the entire body. Before people can truly identify with who they are, they will have to pass through one or two challenges. One part of self-awareness is the ability to discover what needs to be done to take care of oneself. A person will have to grow and evolve around it. Thus, there are everyday activities a person needs to do to live a meaningful and wonderful life.

The other part of self-awareness is what we conceive as human, and these are the things we must do no matter how much we want to resist. An example of this kind of self-awareness is our willingness to take on a job we hate doing so that we can pay our bills. Also, we sometimes discover ourselves through what is forced upon us. For instance, you might not understand what you are capable of doing until you have to do it. Discovering oneself is not an easy task and is one of the hardest things that you need and will have to do to live a meaningful life.

The road to self-awareness is not easy because it occurs in stages. There is a stage at which we blame everyone for whatever we are going through. During this stage, people will never take a lead; all they do is follow. They don't take on any responsibility.

Another stage in self-awareness is taking the blame. This is one of the difficult stages of self-awareness someone can live through because people usually think that whatever happened is their fault. Some may also refuse to take responsibility for whatever happens, even if they have only a tiny role in it, and they usually have low self-esteem.

As people start to gain self-esteem, they decide to partially take responsibility; their feelings start to get better, and the burden on them has typically been subdued.

The next stage of self-awareness is the ability to understand what being responsible is and then being ready to embrace it. It means understanding the concept of reality and not passing the blame on to anyone else. This is when people understand the true meaning of self-awareness, and they see themselves as a big deal—not afraid to take responsibility and use the resources around them correctly.

Generally, Africans need to wake up to be aware of the resources laying dominantly around them and make it work for the development of the continent. The abovementioned point can also help the African community to wake up and become self-aware.

Collective Awareness

Collective awareness is not what you do for others but what you do for yourself. Collective awareness is the ability to make people around you understand who they are and what they can do to get better. Therefore, whatever you do for someone, you are also doing yourself. If people you interact with are conscious of who they are, it will be a betterment for you and the people around you.

The kind of people around you will determine if things get better or worse for you. The world of people around you revolves around you; thus, you are responsible for whatever happens in your life, whether or not you are conscious of it. As you are responsible for whatever happens around you, everyone around you is also responsible for whatever happens around them. This implies that everyone in a group is responsible for whatever happens in their collective world. The collective awareness and cooperation of people around you will determine how a nation and a family prosper. Natural disasters and war can also influence the prosperity and cooperation of a nation.

If you work with people who have vast knowledge about collective awareness, you will see results within a short period. This means you should awaken the consciousness of collective awareness in the people around you. It will be of immense help not only to you but also to the people around you. The wider network of people you build will determine your access to the resources around you.

Resources will multiply when they are distributed because they will increase the value of the people around you. Before you can get ahead, you will have to first help the people around you get ahead. You will rise when you help others rise. The result you get in life is influenced by the collective awareness, either positively or negatively. For instance, if people around you are harming each other and you decide to be passive, this will negatively affect you.

Consider yourself as a being and see the people around you as an extension of yourself, seeing everyone around you as one body and mind. If a part of the body is harmed, it will affect all other parts of the body. Ensure you look after all parts equally. We are one big organism, and if a part dies, every other part of the body goes down with it.

Although it is important to look after others and also take care of their needs, don't do this at the expense of ignoring your own needs. It is not a wise decision to sacrifice one's own well-being to satisfy others. Using a body as an example, if a heart has to sacrifice itself for the brain, both are meaningless.

Collective awareness is knowing that the good of people around you is linked to your good as well, and the two are inseparable. Make sure the decision you make will improve not only your well-being but also the well-being of people around you, simultaneously. When you awaken the awareness of people around you, they will become better, and, in turn, you will too. The world can be a better place for everyone to live only when we all work together to get better.

Self-Preservation

Self-preservation is the foundation of joy and happiness. One cannot give what they don't have, that is, your state of mind, your spiritual life, and your emotional energy are determined by what you will go back to. These are ways you can preserve yourself:

- Stop worrying: Discover what makes you worry, and remove it from your life. Be focused, know what you want, and go for it. Nurture your thoughts carefully as every thought that comes to our mind is like a seed. How we nourish it will determine if it germinates or withers. Worry starts to set in after we find ourselves in certain circumstances, such as loss of job, loss of loved ones, and other types of loss. Worry is like the weed that surrounds our seeds and can hinder them from growing. Therefore, to make the seed grow, we will have to get rid of worry. When you do that, creative thought will set in.

- Make room for creative thoughts: Whenever you encounter a problem, the first thing that should come to your mind is how you can turn it to your good. Look for a way out and ask yourself questions like:
- What am I missing?
- What do I need to try out?
- Who can I call for help?

Asking yourself questions can cultivate a creative thought and bring out the creativity in you. When you finally find yourself in the creative realm, your thoughts will change, and you will start ignoring the closed doors and focus on the open ones.

- Work on your best ideas: All the creative thoughts you come up with will become ideas. Carefully choose the best among those ideas and work on them. You don't need to have all the answers or connections; all you have to do is work on those ideas and make them powerful. When you start working on them, all other resources you need to execute will follow.

Keep in mind that two things usually deprive us from getting what we want. The first one is seeking approval and waiting for permission from people around us. The second one is the thought that it's selfish to go for what we want.

Have you not taken action on what you want because you are thinking of what other people will say about you? Have you given up on your dream because of what your spouse, parents, or a friend might tell you? Thinking about this might keep you stuck for a long period. Therefore, make up your mind and pursue your dream. If you see something that excites you or makes you happy, don't wait for people's approval before you go for it.

Collective Preservation

Unlike self-preservation, collective preservation is the ability to work together as a family, or a community, to live a better life. This is the idea of working together as a team to achieve a specific purpose. Self-preservation has to do with having a powerful thought as an individual and working toward it to become better in life. Collective preservation, on the other hand, has to do with helping and lifting each other up to achieve a set goal.

If you are the only one who is self-preserving in your family or community, it will still affect you. It's like being the only person getting rich in a family of six people who aren't. All other members of the family will depend on you, and before you know it, you will go bankrupt.

No one is an island. We need to hold hands with other people to achieve what we want in life. To achieve greater things in life, consider these two things: the first is the type of friends you move with, which can either make or mar you. Some people have taken a wrong step because of the company they choose, but if you are privileged enough to be self-preserved, you can be the light among your peer group. You can make them see life from your perspective, and they too will start to live a normal life.

The second is the kind of network you build. Human networking has helped a lot of people grow and quickly excel in life. If you are privileged to have connections with famous and wealthy people, it won't take long before you make it. Your journey in life will move faster. Those people you connect with, who help you attain certain achievements in life because they have undergone self-preservation and are lending a helping hand, also help you to grow with them. You, too, need to help someone else do the same. If we keep building those types of connections, this world will be a better place for us all.

Self-Liberation

Self-liberation is the process of living and understanding the true authenticity of self. There are stages to self-liberation, and each one represents the road of overcoming suffering.

To be liberated is to be free from feelings of guilt, shame, hurt, pain, regrets, and anything else that keeps our hearts and souls in bondage. Liberation also allows us the freedom to experience joy, happiness, peace, contentment, and anything else that feeds our mind, body, and spirit.

I would imagine that we are all in pursuit of living a life that makes us feel liberated. However, self-liberation does not happen overnight; nor does it happen in a vacuum. It also doesn't mean that we will never feel sadness, anger, or pain. What it does mean is that you will be aware so that you can be intentional about how it impacts you. To be self-liberated, one must go through the process of self-awareness and self-preservation, both of which are mentioned above. Self-liberation is a journey; there is no end to your process, except for the time at one's death. And then—even in death—there is a freedom, being liberated from the cares and stresses of the world.

When you are liberated, you have clarity of mind, thoughts, and actions. There is acceptance of self and others without judgment. You work on cultivating the joy of being and of doing for yourself and for others without sacrificing who you are and your inner peace. Self-liberation promotes an understanding of grace and gratitude.

You acknowledge the past, but you don't live there; you don't dwell on what happened, or what could have been. You can move toward your present self and present reality. You stay clear of the what-if's, the thoughts of the worst-case scenarios, and the fear of uncertainty. You understand that uncertainty is part of life and that "it is what it is." It's about knowing the true essence of your existence. Liberation allows you to be here now.

Another important aspect of becoming self-liberated is to believe that you have it within you to do it...to behave in ways that align with your true authentic self and to continue the path of transforming into the person you aspire to be. This is the higher stage of freedom. It's the invincible stage that happens in the mind of the liberated individual who starts growing; it is the moment where you start to take more responsibility for what you do, and realize that you are self-liberating—that is, growing from ignorance to knowledge.

As you move through the process of self-liberation, this is where you decide to start living your own life. It requires no explanations, and you enjoy full freedom. At this stage, you are aware of all the challenges you went through from the start and can reflect on your life and determine you have developed internal freedom. You are free to continue to develop and transform yourself every day by empowering yourself and moving from being dependent to independent to interdependent.

Collective Liberation

Collective liberation is coming together as a family or as a community to achieve a greater cause together. As self-liberation generally means freedom, how can we come together as a family or community to get freedom from the oppressors around us? In African culture, a father is regarded to be the head of the family, which implies that the father is expected to provide food, shelter, and security for other members of the family. Therefore, if the security of such a family is threatened, the father will be responsible for it.

The kind of community you see today is determined by how the members of the community are being raised; this is why the psychological well-being of a child cannot be left out. To mentally liberate a child from being oppressed by their peers requires the collective work from both parents. Collective liberation starts from the family before it gradually moves to the community. A community can think of getting liberated only if it can work together. For instance, in Africa most of the community usually comes together to provide for their needs. The first stage of community liberation is to realize what such a community is lacking, which could be a school, electricity, good roads, water, etc. After realizing what they lack in the community, in the next stage, people come together to find solutions to it.

Most of the time, the community members will come together or choose a representative from each of the communities. The representatives will be the ones to give the members of the community feedback. From there, they start to contribute money to execute the project that will provide what they lack. Sometimes, a project is beyond the capacity of the community; this is when the community leader will invite external bodies like government agencies or community-based nonprofit organizations to assist them in executing the project.

Collective liberation is realizing what a community is lacking, coming together to understand the needs, and providing a lasting solution. As Black Caribbean people, we must understand that we have a certain privilege—the privilege of growing up in a place where everyone looked like us. Our teachers were Black, our politicians were Black, and our doctors, our nurses, and our business leaders were Black. Therefore, we had role models we looked up to. However, many African Americans did not have what we had, so we must be compassionate and empathetic and not let our privilege get in the way of coming together as a collective.

COLLECTIVE CARE DIAGRAM (Crump Swaby 2021)

Self-Liberation
Self-liberation is the process of living and understanding the true authenticity of self

Self-Preservation
Self-preservation is the foundation of joy and happiness

Self-Awareness
Self-awareness is the ability to know one's worth and remove the doubt of who one is

Collective Liberation
Collective liberation is coming together as a family or as a community to achieve a greater cause

Collective Preservation
Collective preservation is the ability to work together as a family or community to live a better life

Collective Awareness
Collective awareness is the ability to make people around you understand who they are and what they can do to get better

Healing doesn't mean you'll never get triggered again, or that eventually you're going to arrive somewhere free of any pain or suffering. Healing is a quiet homecoming. It's about returning to yourself and settling peacefully into the truth of who you are. Not incomplete, not broken. Whole, lovable, human.

Unknown

CHAPTER 10

PASSING THE BATON:
A LEGACY OF HEALING

"In order to heal others, we first need to heal ourselves. And to heal ourselves, we need to know how to deal with ourselves"
~Thic Nhat Han

"Create your legacy and pass the baton."
~Billie Jean King

Billie Jean King might not have been born African American, but she definitely knows a thing or two about prejudice, stereotypes, and fighting to create a legacy of success. She had supported gender equality and social justice for decades and struck a massive blow for women's rights when, at age 29, she destroyed masochistic male tennis player Bobby Riggs in the legendary "Battle of the Sexes" tennis match. King knew it wasn't enough to just get on even footing for herself, but she also had to pay it forward, which is something that Blacks must do as they come into their own and start to heal from trauma. What good does it do us to heal ourselves from the trauma we have inherited, if we don't find and use the tools necessary to equip those who come after us with the power to do likewise?

As you flip through the pages of this book, you may find that it compels you to not only want to transform, but to transform the lives of the people you love and care for. When you approach them, though, they may or may not be interested in what you have to say. They may even prefer to remain the way they are. You may think, *why don't they want better?* The question is, is it that they don't want better, or is it that they are not aware of what they need in order to want better? I honestly believe it's the latter. An article in *Psychology Today*, "Deepening Your Awareness of Unawareness," states, "The greatest obstacle to awareness is the fact that our interactions with the world consist of us projecting our concept of reality onto everything and everyone. Until you understand the basic nature of this process, there are no alternatives. Our abstract thinking is embedded in our brains as deeply as any physical object or sensation. It is how we make sense of life and is our version of reality." ("Deepening Your Awareness of Unawareness | Psychology Today" n.d.)

It is my belief that we all want better, and what we know as better is all we know until awareness is present. In life we all start from a place of being unaware, and therefore we move through life wearing the lens of unawareness. This unawareness, until tapped into, is where we will continue to stay and possibly feel comfortable staying because we don't know something deeper is within. Therefore, your work cannot be their work. Each person must come to their own awareness. The most you can do is to work on yourself with the hopes that if they see your transformation happening, they too will begin to look inward and become aware of the unconscious beliefs and ways they have been existing in the world.

As we transform and heal, we might experience the "curse of knowledge," which is the belief that once we know something, we assume everyone else knows it too. However, that's the cognitive dissonance we may need to release. On the other hand, the person who chooses not to do better experiences the "status quo bias," where they tend to prefer things to stay the same because any change from the baseline is a loss—a loss that is too painful to sit with. Many people are not opposed to change; they are opposed to the loss they will experience because of the change. And in anything, and almost all things, grieving any kind of loss is painful. We put up a protective wall that blocks our ability for others to see our true selves, and all the while, the same wall is blocking our ability to become aware of the areas in our lives that need to be transformed. Is it that they don't want better? I think not. It is the unawareness of not knowing there is something better or knowing there is something better but being unaware of how to or what to do to obtain it.

To be aware, we must be aware of our unawareness. This process brings us into our present selves so that we can nurture the parts of us that are keeping us in bondage. If we would only connect with our past, grieve the loss, and move toward acceptance and forgiveness, the pain will begin to lessen. If we look at it from a place of Christianity or spirituality, it's in some ways saying that we can't be in accordance with our lives unless we yield to the will of God or a higher power, and therein we're free to live a life fully and embodied.

Then there's the entitlement mentality of those who feel as though the world or the people around them owe them something. So they either take without asking or just keep taking because they feel it's their right. These are observed behaviors and attitudes from history. Many of the slaves owners operated from this mindset. Of course, there are times when we need to reach back and bring forth those who have been left behind, but this is different from them believing or expecting it because they have a right to what you have accomplished.

This way of being can be attributed to the brainwashing or conditioning our ancestors experienced while being enslaved. The belief that if the master was sick, *we all sick.* If the master is happy, *we all happy.* Our ancestors were forced to take on the feelings, thoughts, behaviors, and emotions of the slave master. The "what's mine is mine" and "what's yours is mine" mentality is subconsciously still at work.

We also continue to have "property" mentality. It's an unconscious burden we bare on both sides. People who work hard, and by any means necessary, to build a life for themselves and their families may experience guilt for doing good and doing better for themselves.

Then there are those people who sit back and expect to benefit from others to build the life they want for themselves. As we know, this country was built on the backs, blood, sweat, and tears of our ancestors. We poured into this country only to be rewarded with racism, discrimination, poverty, and oppression. This is part of the belief and behaviors that are passed down generationally via conditioning. Many have developed passive and aggressive beliefs and values that are buried deep in our subconscious and keep us chained to them. This conditioning has made us believe we are entitled to each other's successes and whatever else comes with it. We turn on our own instead of shifting the responsibility to where it really belongs. This is what historical trauma response does; it keeps us chained to the oppressor. Therefore, we hold on to the values, beliefs, and behaviors of the oppressor because it's safe and too scary to unlock a system that has been in bondage for so long.

It must be a cultural practice, meaning that it goes beyond ourselves and beyond our families. The foundational changes of embracing the positive legacies of our past must be built into creating new legacies, starting with our own successes. We can't just attend therapy and expect the lessons we learn to turn into a new way of doing things for ourselves and others. Changing a culture's belief system takes patience, trust, and, above all else, resilience to rise above the shortcomings of previous generations and build a new foundation for future generations to stand upon.

Part of building that resilience is the knowledge that everyone has a greater purpose to fulfill in the community beyond their own sense of individual value. For instance, older people might feel that they are without purpose once they retire and move to live in a senior citizen community because they are no longer contributing to a work environment or making money to pay bills for family members. But their children step in to remind them that they still have an incredibly valuable role as grandparents—lending support to grandchildren as a source of wisdom, of love, of compassion, and more.

Older generations of Blacks might feel the same way, that the trauma they carry makes them too damaged to contribute anything to future generations when it comes to healing. But like the example above, it is just the opposite. Resilience does not come about by being stoic or aloof but through action, through sharing, and through conversations that break us free from the shackles of downplaying trauma and allow others to see our pain, frustration, and how we have taken strides to escape the past and create our own legacy based on self-empowerment and the belief that what was is not a reflection of what is or what can be.

Authentic Communication

Imagine two Black friends meet for dinner on a Sunday night. One has just been laid off from her job due to cutbacks from COVID-19; the other is struggling to keep a failing marriage together and her oldest child from heading toward a life of crime and gang activity that seems to be her child's current career choice. When the two greet each other and settle into a conversation, neither one dares bring up her troubles to the other. The conversation is light and breezy, full of laughs and common sayings, a cadence of comparing gossip; talking about the Black experience (or the struggle in general); revisiting old, shared memories; and generally deflecting the conversation for the entire course of their dinner from what's really going on in their lives. What's with all the deception? Why can't either of them let their guard down and let one another see that they are struggling and in pain?

The burden of Black culture weighs heavily on both friends. The fear of showing weakness outside of one's own home is prevalent—like the worry of looking like a failure, like life has beaten them down, like they can't handle their own business. It's all part of the debilitating mindset that keeps trauma passing from one generation to another, instead of stopping the cycle with honesty, transparency, and the ability to admit needing help and openly asking for support inside the Black community. Authentic communication begins with being our authentic self when communicating both internally and externally. This means talking in our own voice and using vocabulary that expresses what we truly mean, think, and feel, instead of adopting a persona that we think reflects us in the best light based on what we perceive as accepted behavior by our social circle.

Let's look at a second example. Imagine a Black teenage male, whose girlfriend recently cheated on him. His heart hurts, and he feels inadequate, but he pushes those feelings deep down inside when he talks to his peer group or to older Black males about the situation. He has grown up surrounded by male role models who treat women as inferior, objects to be used and then tossed aside when done, and definitely not worth heartache, tears, or even a second thought when the relationship is done. Those built-in perceptions keep the young man from being able to practice self-love and, in the process, uncover his authentic voice. While he might be hurting inside, he believes that revealing those feelings to anyone else will result in him being mocked and seen as weak, and cause others to disassociate from him.

What this young man needs is the conscious leadership of those in his community who have experienced their own trauma and have made the decision to break free from that degenerative cycle and create their own legacy. That doesn't mean they won't experience downtimes, heartache, and regret. It does mean that they will embrace all of those emotions, stop trying to bury them deep down, and stop identifying solely by the plight of those who came before them. Without people who are willing to not only break this cycle but communicate how and why to do it to younger generations, their work will only be a blip on the radar…an isolated incident in the continuing struggle of Black people, instead of a new foundational event that future generations build a brighter, healthier future upon.

Being able to have that kind of communication with others has to start with internal communication. If we don't think these things are healthy and appropriate, how can we express them to others and develop ourselves into leaders who can serve as guideposts for those who will look to us to show the way? It is not far off from learning a new language altogether, as we will recalibrate our tone when speaking on our emotions. This involves changing our tone and using new expressions of both verbal and nonverbal communication to invite dialogue and sharing and openness. This must be an intentional, continuous process in which we are both teacher and student, continuing to reflect on what we are experiencing and how we are relating to others—a process of self that will last a lifetime. This is not just a psychological experience but a spiritual one as well. So many Blacks are powerful Christians who pray regularly to God and believe wholeheartedly in the miracle of Jesus Christ, but don't seem to follow the examples he laid down in the Bible when it comes to being the good neighbor, the good brother or sister, or a person who makes it his or her mission to uplift community in good times and in bad.

Generational Wealth

By definition, our ancestors who spent their lives as slaves had no money, no possessions, and no homes to call their own except that which was given to them by their masters. We live in different times —times in which we own property, run our own businesses, get promoted, can afford to take vacations and buy gifts for our loved ones, and express ourselves through our purchases and lifestyle choices. We are not the first generation of Blacks to do this. But we continue to contextualize our existence in terms of the struggles of our ancestors, even if no one in living memory has battled against hunger or homelessness or the inability to provide for their own family.

For many of us, we are unaware of the fact that there have been generations of successful Blacks who have come before us. We continue to subscribe to the narrative that we are destined to make less money than Whites, work less-important jobs, and live in poorer neighborhoods simply because that is the way the world works and that is the way our ancestors lived. Dreaming beyond our limitations never occurs for many of us because it is embedded in our DNA that rising to financial and societal prominence is a dangerous proposition. This belief system is examined in the OWN network documentary series "The Legacy of Black Wall Street" that debuted in the summer of 2021.

A century ago, Oklahoma's Greenwood District was a 36-block development that housed many affluent Black professionals during the oil and mineral boom of the era. There were Black attorneys, entrepreneurs, real estate agents, and doctors, along with Black-owned grocery stores, barbershops, a funeral home, and more. What looked like a utopia for Blacks fewer than 60 years after the end of the Civil War became a living nightmare. A young Black man accused of assaulting a young White woman was jailed, starting a confrontation between armed groups of Black and White men around the jail over whether or not he would be lynched.

That confrontation ended in gunfire with twelve people dead, and mobs of Whites formed throughout Tulsa, many of them deputized by the sheriff's department, and set loose to destroy Greenwood. By the end of the 36-hour reign of terror, 10,000 Blacks were homeless; the equivalence of $33 million worth of damage (in today's money) had been done, the death toll varied between 75 and 300 people, and as many as 6,000 Blacks were interred in holding facilities throughout Tulsa for several days for the sole reason that they were Black. This horrific event formed the foundation for Blacks across the country that doing good for themselves would lead to their ruin. The fact that the city of Tulsa and the state of Oklahoma largely omitted the massacre from written history only cemented the fact.

OWN's documentary has taken a step in the right direction by not focusing the series on the massacre, but on the people who built and flourished on Black Wall Street and comparing them to leading Black entrepreneurs of today who are proving that there are no limitations holding us back from succeeding in all things. It is not a process that a TV network should have to take on alone, however. As a culture, we must embrace the positives of the past instead of focusing only on those events that we feel beat us down so badly that we will never recover and don't want to try to overcome. Our wealth does not exist merely in terms of money, but in our talents and intelligence and abilities. In the era of slavery, Black parents would often downplay their children's intelligence, strength, or other particular abilities because they feared that if their White owners became aware of such traits, they would sell the children elsewhere and they'd never be seen again.

Even in our modern culture, this fear of recognition exists in our DNA. We might brag on our daughter's intelligence or our son's natural athletic gifts in our own family, but in mixed company we downplay their gifts for fear that they—and, largely by extension, we—will be seen as threats to Whites, a mindset that historical traumas like the Tulsa massacre only stoke the flames of, even a century later.

Sharing Stories of Liberation

How do we change the narrative of what the Black experience is for our generation and those to come? By sharing stories of power, freedom, resilience, and opportunity that showcase the best of us and the best of our past.

When our children go to school to learn history, as has been mentioned earlier in this book, Black people are vaguely mentioned in prehistory, then omitted until the slave trade becomes prominent in the 1600 and 1700s as European explorers began settling North, Central, and South America with their colonies and "conquered" African nations to provide slave labor and servants for their new sections of empire. Rarely is it written that these explorers were, in fact, invaders, taking over land that had belonged to Native Americans for thousands of years, taking what they wanted based on superior firepower and strength in numbers, and slaughtering the natives if they dared stand against their expansion plans.

Equally disturbing is that for Black children (in public school), their introduction to their own race is as property, slaves, or chattel who were taken from their homes by force, shoved onto ships to live in squalor for weeks or months, then put in shackles and sold to strangers in a land they had never seen who spoke a language they had never heard. Is it any wonder our young people struggle so much to find their identities when that is what they are taught at school from the moment they are first introduced to what history is?

While Whites are lauded for their accomplishments dating back hundreds of years, Blacks are rarely mentioned by name in history books until at least the 19th century. Where is the history for us to be proud of? Must we center it all on our accomplishments of the last 160 years, a drop in the bucket in the history of our race?

What about the Moors, who ruled parts of Spain and Portugal for 700 years as kings and queens? What about the fact that human history actually began in Africa according to all archaeological research? What about the fact that Ta- Seti, in Sudan, is believed to be the first organized state in human history? What about the fact that great king-doms existed in Africa before the year 1500 that had taken part in international trading and foreign relations with the likes of India and China, participating in trans-oceanic travel in the process? Just because these stories have been muted and whitewashed by history books doesn't mean they didn't exist. We can combat this system of misinformation by decentering Whiteness and recentering Blackness in our own lives, changing the narrative that only wants to see the lives of Blacks starting in slavery.

This is an uphill climb, but there are Black academics around the world willing to challenge it:

"When you start with slavery, you're actually starting history with pain," says Cilas Kemedjio, director of the Frederick Douglass Insti-tute at the University of Rochester. "You're starting as if the story of Black people started with slavery. People who are more inclined to the Afrocentric, they will generally start with the history of Egypt that Black people built the pyramids."

Educating ourselves on the true origins of Black history, tracing our own family roots back beyond the slave days to where we originated from—whether that is Africa, the Caribbean, or somewhere else—and holding ourselves accountable in letting go of the things that no longer serve us in a positive manner are all foundational steps to self-liberation from the effects of intergenerational and historical trauma. Look around your home, look around your life, and look around your community; realize all of the amazing contributions that our Black ancestors, whether they be American, African, Caribbean, or Latino, have brought forward into our modern lives. These are things to be celebrated and honored and shared, not hidden out of sight. Being a smaller population than Whites does not make our history, our accomplishments, our traditions, and our values any less important.

Passing the Baton

When we apply our thought process to the situation, the questions of "why" we need to create our own legacy and pass that baton forward to future generations are easy to answer. Understanding the process of 'how' is a bit more complex, as we have seen in these previous few chapters. While it takes dedication, resilience, and the ability to reframe our thoughts and words and actions, it also takes introspection on creating a process that will assist us in succeeding in this mission.

The following reflective questions can provide you with the framework to develop your own pathway to finding the good parts of our past and combining them with the positives of the present to build the new legacy of being Black.

1. **In what ways has your past influenced your present?**
   Make sure you limit your answers to your specific past—the life you have lived and the experiences unique to you and

during your own lifetime—without confusing them with things that happened to your relatives or ancestors. Be specific and intentional. These questions should be answered in written format, so that you can reflect back on the answers at any time and build upon them. Use the journal pages at the end of the book and be sure to include both positives and negatives in the events of your past.

2. **What are you willing to let go of?** You might consider this the million-dollar question in starting to form your own legacy. These include things in your past that are weighing you down; the things you have inherited from your parents, their parents, and other relatives; and the things that are part of Black culture—whether or not you are aware of them. These things can and will hurt you, but you don't have to let them. You don't have to give away control of your life. You can consciously announce that you are not letting these negative things keep command of you, whether it be the specter of slavery and the inherent fear of doing things that call attention to yourself like the power of addictions, a cycle of abandonment or abuse, or anything else that you do not want to define your life anymore.

3. **What can you hold on to?** Just as important as letting go of the detriments to your legacy is holding on to the positives that have shaped your life through your ancestors—think about things like religious conviction, work ethic, and the strength of the family and community, as well as things that bring you joy (i.e., traditions like singing and dancing or giant family gatherings after church on Sundays).

4. **What is the legacy you want to leave?** When you can separate yourself from the negatives that have previously defined you, you will realize that your legacy resembles a blank slate, a fresh canvas waiting for you to splash colorful,

vibrant strokes across and paint the picture that represents your life. This is your opportunity to connect with your past, grieve over the losses that linger there, and move toward acceptance and forgiveness. It involves educating ourselves on the positives of what our Black community and ancestors have given to us and continuing the legacy of our ancestors by sharing what we know. When we change the narrative, we can change our circumstances.

It goes without saying that I love my family, and I love my children. I realize that it's my responsibility to leave a legacy of honesty, truth, and authenticity for them. It's my responsibility to let go of the burdens I've carried and the burdens I've picked up throughout my lifetime, and to work toward releasing them. Why? Because my children should not have to carry the weight of my shame, my anger, my guilt, my anxiety, or anything else that may keep them chained.

It is I who must create a legacy that is filled with joy, excitement, love, sympathy, and compassion. They must know that rage, dishonesty, fear and whatever else that keeps them chained serves no purpose. Yes, these feelings may arise, but they need not stay and take up space in your heart, mind, your body, or your soul. Bring awareness to them, acknowledge them, welcome them in, and thank them for showing up, but do not let them occupy space. Let them go.

You are also built on the legacy of resilience, strength, wealth, intelligence, spirituality, commitment, and togetherness. It's your responsibility to cultivate these legacies and pass them on too.

You are being presented with a choice:
evolve or remain. If you choose to remain
unchanged, you will be presented with the
same challenges, the same routine, the same
storms, the same situations, until you learn
from them, until you love yourself enough
to say "no more", until you choose change.
If you choose to evolve, you will connect
with the strength within you, you will explore
what lies outside the comfort zone,
you will awaken to love, you will become,
you will be. You have everything you need.
Choose to evolve. Choose love.

- creig crippen -

A New Beginning

"Change will not come if we wait for some other person or some other time. We are the ones we've been waiting for. We are the change that we seek."
~ President Barack Obama

"Plant a seed. Grow a tree. Bear good fruits. And, leave a legacy. It's what this generation needs."
~ Gayl Crump Swaby

Change does not come without pain. If it did, every one of us would have cast aside those invisible shackles long ago and banished our ghosts with a mere thought. We would have transformed grief into joy and pain into love. But we know it doesn't work that way. In fact, that's perhaps the most common reason why we struggle to change our mindsets and conquer our pasts.

The idea of having to go through painful self-analysis and cathartic healing is not something many of us have the courage to accomplish.

There's no doubting our willpower; we've been proving our strength in that regard for generations. But fear of the unknown, fear of condemnation from our own social and family circles, and fear of reliving past trauma stunt our growth time and again. What will tomorrow look like as we take this journey together to mitigate the effects of personal, historical, and intergenerational trauma?

Know that trauma will never stop happening to us on a multitude of levels. It is an unfortunate part of human nature and the environment we live in. The world is flawed, and despite our best efforts, support systems, and own mental willpower, we are simply not equipped with the mental ability to cope with every event that befalls us. And those results can be such a mental, neurological, or physical manifestation.

In our new frame of mind and way of thinking, we do not shy away from our traumas, or seek to downplay or bury them. Whether the symptoms of trauma come immediately or over time, we address them; we seek out help with coping with them, and we break the cycle of allowing them to become relational or letting them consume our lives. This is a great plan of attack for our personal traumas, but what about the historical ones that have been weighing on our families and our race as a whole for decades—sometimes, even centuries?

Recall that historical trauma is the remembered mental representation of a wounding event that is shared across the passage of time; it's complex because it is a collective experience. As we have discussed at length, slavery and the Reconstruction that followed are the leading examples of this for Blacks in America, but not the only ones. Black residents of Memphis, Tennessee have reported historical trauma from residing in the city where Martin Luther King, Jr. was assassinated in 1968. Blacks in Tulsa, Oklahoma, identify with the historical trauma of the 1921 Tulsa Massacre that was largely covered up and omitted from history books for close to a century.

We overcome this sort of legacy burden by separating those who came before us from who we are now and recognizing that the positives of their lives are much more vital to shaping ours than the negatives. We are not our ancestors, familial or otherwise. The degradations and suffering they experienced are reminders of where we came from, not identifying marks of who we must be.

While it is not always the source of historical trauma, the forced tragedy of slavery has prolonged effects on Blacks in the United States for hundreds of years, and we accept it. The intentional attempt of dehumanizing a group of people based solely on the color of their skin is not a wound that ever heals completely, and the scars remain—visible or not. As painful as that history is, we must use it as a learning tool, not a crutch on which to continue believing we are not smart enough, strong enough, wealthy enough, or free enough to realize our own dreams.

Our slave ancestors might have been denied the ability to gain an education, but we do not use this as an excuse to stay illiterate or unaware. Their families were broken up by the White man's law. We, however, do not have to live in broken homes as a result. Slave owners attacked the Black family structure to divide and conquer. We are 150 years clear of these monstrous practices. We know we are stronger together, so why do we intentionally fracture ourselves?

The third type of trauma we must contend with is intergenerational trauma, which is more intimate in that it revolves around patterns of suffering, abuse, and struggles that people directly related to us have experienced: patterns of behavior such as physical abuse, divorce, addiction in any form, depression, and so forth. We also must be aware that trauma isn't always one specific event, but can take the form of micro-traumas—things that happen chronically over time and eventually topple us with their collective weight. This is a type of trauma on which we cannot begin to build our own legacy and our own family history until we mentally and psychologically extricate ourselves from the mistakes, illnesses, and circumstances of our parents, grandparents, and other near relations. We are not them, any more than they were their own parents, and that is a tough lesson to unlearn when we have been indoctrinated since childhood to believe things like alcoholism, physical abuse, and broken homes are not only accepted but simply "the way things are."

As we grow older and become aware of the world around us and see things through the lens of our own experience, we must strive to do better—individually and as a community. Accepting what happened in the past is not our way, no more than it was in the era of slavery, Reconstruction, Jim Crow, or during the Civil Rights era of the 1950s and 1960s; no more than it is today when we see police brutality against our brothers and sisters that is perpetrated for no better a reason than the color of their skin juxtaposed to that of the officers'. The legacy of what came before us must not burden what we will become nor what we will create for those who come after us.

The word "legacy" is defined as "something transmitted by or received from an ancestor or predecessor or from the past." Through the tools we have cultivated in this book, we can begin the transition away from the burdens of legacy that have been passed down generationally and historically from our own families and from our BIPOC heritage. We can instead begin shaping our own legacy of positives that we hope to pass on to the generations to come, not only our blood relatives but also members of the communities we are active in, by showing what it means to be Black in America. This intergenerational belief is that what happened in one generation will influence what happens in the next, for good or ill. Values, myths, fantasies, and beliefs will transcend time and circumstances.

There is rigorous, intentional, and often challenging work to be done here. It is not the work of a few therapy sessions, a weekend-long seminar, or even a 12-step program. It is changing our beliefs, our thought patterns, the way we view ourselves, the way we view others, how we communicate, and, most importantly, how we love ourselves. Both the good and not-so-good parts of us comprise our whole.

As we have said previously, but I feel it is so very important to reiterate, we are not in pursuit of perfection here. There is only one being in this entire universe who exemplifies perfection, and He does not need to read this book! We are not trying to rid ourselves of emotions like grief, anger, sadness, and frustration either. Those are all natural emotions that are part of the very core of what makes us human. Our objective is to gain the wisdom, understanding, and ability to recognize, categorize, and work through those emotions in a healthy way that prevents the personal trauma we do encounter from engulfing us in the present or in the future.

Additionally, we can learn to recognize the traumas that don't belong to us, but which we believe we have inherited anyway, and begin the process of separating past from present, fact from fiction, and negative burdens from positive legacies, in order to embrace the contributions our ancestors have passed onto us, without shackling ourselves and taking on their heavy burdens again and again.

Our legacy burdens, also known as ancestral burdens, can take the form of feelings, beliefs, energies, and behaviors. Many of us hold on to these burdens and our traumas even without being aware of them, letting them take up space in our minds, hearts, souls, and spirits. They are not open wounds in our flesh that are easily diagnosed. They are often caused by epigenetics, the transferring of trauma across generations through the genes of an already traumatized person. For example, this is what allows post-traumatic stress disorder (PTSD) to be passed down from parent to child.

As we become aware of such possessions, which we would seemingly like to throw in the trash, we often find they are not so easily removed. Beliefs, habits, and views of ourselves that we know to be negative are not so quickly cast aside when they are all we know and what we have grown used to, comfortable with, or even reliant upon. The single Black mother who trusts no man and fuels her anger into protecting her family and powering her work ethic might make that solution work in the short term, but over time, the anger will turn to bitterness, and when her children are grown and gone, what will she have left to work for?

If her father abandoned her family during her childhood, or her husband did likewise early in her adult life, she must fight her way through the inclinations she will face that say she is unworthy of love and/or that men cannot be trusted to provide love or support for their families. As Black people, we tend to hold on to our inherited thoughts, behaviors, and beliefs, even when they are killing us on the inside. We succumb to negative emotions like hatred, mistrust, and bitterness because they fit our narrative of self-loathing, and feeling unlovable and devalued by our own families and by society as a whole.

Traditions of Black culture tend to grow over time, often to the detriment of those who are part of it and often deviating so significantly from God's word and plan that it becomes unrecognizable. The more we shutter these negative feelings and thoughts inside ourselves, the more we suffer needlessly, and the more likely future generations will suffer after we are gone. We have the tools available to change this path, for ourselves and future generations, but it must start with the courage to look in the mirror and tell yourself that you deserve better, as was said in a song by the late Michael Jackson, "Man in the Mirror."

Need I remind you, in family therapy, "the first generation inflicts trauma, the next generation goes into recovery, and hopefully, the third generation is spared." This is the journey of infliction to healing to release, but for many Blacks, healing and release never come. We praise ourselves on our ability to endure suffering, pain, and despair and emerge stronger at the end of it. But is all that internal pain making us stronger? Or beating us down to the point that we lose the battle before it's ever even fought?

While our ancestors had physical barriers in place that kept them from aspiring beyond their current conditions, most of our barriers are self-imposed and take root inside of us. Modern BIPOC have their own barriers strengthened by a lack of belief in their right to better lives, the malaise of time, and a lack of education on mental health and healing. This process starts from the moment we enter school and begin learning European (White) history that largely omits the history of Africa—where life truly began on Earth—and discounts our greatest minds and cultural contributors. But are we so powerless that we cannot change what is being taught? Any less powerful than we are in deciding what we want to do with our lives?

We are strong people. We know how to organize. We know how to call attention to wrongs in our society, even in ways that are nonviolent. We have many examples of how we have organized in the past and how our ancestors organized. When we see a failing of fundamental teaching about the history of our people in school settings, we have the tools to change it, but only if we make an effort. Assuming someone else will take up the call to action is failing to be a member of our local community and a member of the Black race in general. It is a character flaw shared by members of every ethnic group on this planet. Seeing something wrong and not saying or doing anything about it is tantamount to condoning it.

If we don't become the change we wish to see in the world, how can we expect things to ever get any better? Self-help tools such as giving ourselves permission and understanding the different components of the way we communicate with others, the way we occupy space, and how we align our words can all impact breakthroughs to better mental health and better circumstances.

Our new legacy must begin in the family unit, where specific expectations White for men and women have long existed, due to our traumatic pasts, but must be exorcised in order for us to begin living happy, healthy, and free from the long-ranging effects of trauma. Black women see themselves as strong, which is a great self-view, but when that strength comes at the cost of their own identity, their own healthy release of pain and their own ambitions are quashed so that they must be the family provider from the first hint of adulthood until death; it is a decidedly unhealthy path to take.

Unfortunately, daughters of many of these women see this strong Black woman as their role model and perpetuate it through their own lives, furthering the cycle instead of finding the tools to break it. Push past these barriers and relinquish these burdens. Releasing requires action, and so we must be active participants in this process. This involves using the P.A.U.S.E. Method, which I have explained at length earlier in the text but will touch on lightly again here as a great pathway to a new you. (Return to page 146 for details.) When you are not sure as to what's going on with you, or even when you feel you have been wronged and are ready to react, I invite you to P.A.U.S.E. before taking action.

1. **P**ay attention to what and where you feel it in your body.
2. Accept and acknowledge it, and know that it's okay.
3. Unlock the belief that is holding you hostage.
4. **S**top and sit with the thought, and identify the feeling that comes with the belief.
5. **E**mbrace, engage, and evaluate your relationship to the thought or the feeling.

While P.A.U.S.E. is an acronym, it is not a shortcut to success or freedom. The Black community is more aware of our psychological deficiencies now than at any other time in history. We must break free from the denial that we are without fault and without the burdens that have plagued us for generations in order to provide a better tomorrow for both ourselves and our children and future generations. We do this by committing to an entirely new form of thinking—internally and externally—and going to work with the purpose of finding self-discovery, self-acceptance, and self-love.

This healing takes many forms, starting with the personal traumas, which may be the easiest to recognize but the most difficult to overcome. When we bury that trauma deep or pretend it doesn't bother us, we run the risk of making it far worse over time, to the point where the pain erupts out of us with deadly results. Steps toward healing include being willing to heal, accepting the support of loved ones, getting professional help, practicing mindfulness and meditation, and moving/exercising. Collective traumas are those that damage an entire community. While some of the individual trauma techniques will work here as well, establishing programs to help others and using grief counselors in the community can be a big step forward as well.

For all wounds, exploring and then embracing the positive legacies of your ancestors is an amazing way to connect to the true history of your family and not just focus on the negative and the things you wish had never happened. If your family had not experienced love, success, and joy, you would not be here today! Embrace their accomplishments with pride.

Remember the African concept of UBUNTU, which means "I am because we are." As we grow in self-esteem and self-confidence, our collective awareness blossoms, and we develop the ability to make the people around us understand who they are and what they can do to get better. Resources will multiply and increase the value of the people around you. This is the foundation of how a community heals, grows, and achieves its potential.

When your community is strong, it sets the tempo for the people who join it and the children who are born into it. The only thing more contagious than negative emotions are positive ones. A child born into a family unit and a community where no one feels hope for a brighter tomorrow and everyone is burdened by what happened in the past will struggle mightily to grow beyond those things. But a child born into a family and a community where great things are happening, people are lifting each other up, and trust and fellowship are staples of everyday life will be infused with those positive experiences and have a much better chance to learn from them, succeed via them, and pass them on to the next generations to come.

The foundational changes that embrace the positive legacies of our past must be built to create new legacies, starting with recognizing our successes and passing them down to future generations. We must be resilient, anti-fragile, and realize that while we are affecting change for our future, it is not going to prevent negative things from happening. We will still know grief, pain, anger, sadness, and suffering, but we will have new tools to cope with them and to keep them from consuming us. We will aspire to participate in authentic communication; to build generational wealth; to be emotionally, psychologically, and spiritually wealthy (or well-thee); and to share stories of our liberation. Passing the baton involves creating our own legacy of hope and healing, which we can transmit forward to those who come after us.

About the Author

Gayl Crump Swaby is a Mental Health Consultant, an Associate Professor of Counseling, and an author who is deeply passionate about empowering her diverse range of clients to heal generational trauma and embrace wholeness. As the Founder of New Generation Consultants & Associates, LLC, Gayl is dedicated to offering a radical new approach to trauma-informed treatment and care, and she hopes to inspire her multicultural client base to treat their mental health struggles and enrich their lives. Gayl is the author of *Unlocking Legacies & Releasing Burdens*, and she's traveled across the United States, Africa, and South America to share her message, provide training and consultations, and spread mental health awareness.

Gayl is an Associate Professor of Counseling at Springfield College, and she currently serves as the Program Director for the Clinical Mental Health Counseling Program for their Boston Campus. She currently lives in Boston with her husband and their two wonderful children. In her free time, she enjoys traveling and gardening.

Acknowledgments

This book is written in Loving Memory of my brother, Link Lorne Crump, whose burdens were lifted and released June 7, 2020, and my father, Theophilus Crump, whose burdens were lifted and released October 19, 2010.

First and foremost, I thank God for His goodness and mercies toward me. If it wasn't for Him, I would not be where I am today. I have learned that I can be perfect in my imperfections and that, with Him, *I am enough.* It is said that God rarely puts something new in your life until you let go of something old and broken. If that is true, I am extremely grateful to my husband Carlos Sr. and our two beautiful, amazing, and forgiving children, Carlos Jr. and Kaelyn, who challenge me every day to be a better parent and also provide the inspiration for me to work on releasing my own legacy burdens.

To Ulric, Sonya, Dawn, Eleanor, Yves, Bill, Dena, and Desiree (my TAGV/NewGen family), thank you for the laughter, the conversations, and the regular monthly Monday-night deep discussions.

To my Amali Dream Foundation sistas, my "ride or die" (Donna and Monique), thank you for the late-night Zoom meetings when the pandemic hit…the meetings that lasted five hours, of which we used only 20 minutes for planning and the other 4+ hours for everything else.

To my "Boss" Lourdes Pires, who encouraged me to write by supplying me with a blank journal entitled "Girl, You Are Boss."

Because of you, this book is a reality. Thank you for the encouragement and the extra push.

To Dr. C., thank you for walking me through the midst of the difficult times in my life, being my mental wellness lifeline, and helping me to work toward releasing my burdens and shifting into radical acceptance of my present reality. Also, for your patience, commitment, and undying support while holding space for me, I thank you, and I appreciate you.

To Dee Dale, Linda, Kimberly, and Cassandra, thank you all for believing in me and always supporting me.

To the amazing and extraordinaire editor Ms. Shaundale Rénā (ShaundaleRena.com). From the initial conversation to the final pages, I knew our work together would create a professional bond. You are a rockstar! Your coaching and guidance were instrumental throughout the process, and I thank you for being you and for helping me bring this manuscript to life.

Dr. Edith Frazer, my forever mentor, advisor, and supporter, thank you for your authenticity and for always being available when I call or email.

And finally, to my mother and my siblings, as the youngest of all the living children, I have learned so much about what it means to believe in myself. Thank you for believing in me.

A special shout-out to Julia, Ivelisse, Paula, Elsa, Sharita, Fabienne, Daysa, Tayla, and Karla (the CPLAN crew) and Mama-Advocates, a group of committed, dedicated and phenomenal Black and Brown women who go hard every day in every way to make sure that all children receive a well-rounded quality education, inclusive of their physical, emotional, social, and mental well-being. I am always honored to be in your presence.

CAN YOU HELP?

Thank you for reading *Unlocking Legacies & Releasing Burdens!* I really appreciate all of your feedback, and I love hearing what you have to say. I need your input to make the next version of this book and my future books better. So, please leave me an honest review on Amazon, letting me know what you thought of this book. Thanks so much! And just for you, I've included a playlist that has been instrumental in my healing journey and throughout the writing process.

~Dr. Gayl Crump Swaby

"Can't Give Up Now," Mary Mary

"A Better Day," Eleanor Wright

"Let Go," DeWayne Woods

"Deliver Me," Donald Lawrence & the Tri-City Singers

"God Still Heals," DeWayne Woods

"Grateful," Pastor Hezekiah Walker

"He Has His Hands on Me," Pastor Marvin Sapp

"Break Every Chain," Tasha Cobbs

"There Ain't Nothing," James Fortune

"The Curse Is Broken," James Fortune & FIYA

"Lord You Are Good," Todd Galberth

"I Believe," Jonathan Nelson

"With You," James Fortune &FIYA

"Still," Brian Courtney Wilson

"Life and Favor," John P. Kee

"Many Rivers to Cross," Jimmy Cliff

NOTES

Notes

NOTES

Notes

Notes

NOTES

Notes

NOTES

Notes

Notes

Bibliography

"African American Leaders Unhappy with K-12 Education System; Eager to Make Changes." n.d. UNCF. Accessed February 8, 2022. https://uncf.org/news/African.

"Black and African American Communities and Mental Health." Mental Health America. Accessed January 24, 2022. https://www.mhanational.org/issues/black-african-american-communities-and-mental-health.

"Deepening Your Awareness of Unawareness | Psychology Today." n.d. http://www.psychologytoday.com. Accessed April 20, 2022. https://www.psychologytoday.com/us/blog/anxiety-another-name-pain/202201/deepening-your-awareness-unawareness.

Bloom, Sandra L. 1996. "Every Time History Repeats Itself, the Price Goes Up: The Social Reenactment of Trauma." *Sexual Addiction & Compulsivity* 3 (3): 161–94.
https://doi.org/10.1080/10720169608400111.

Elliott, Mary, Jazmine Hughes, New York Times Magazine August 23, and 2019. n.d. "Brief History of Slavery You Didn't Learn in School | RealClearPolicy." https://www.realclearpolicy.com. Accessed January 26, 2022.
https://www.realclearpolicy.com/2019/08/23/brief_history_of_slavery_you_didn039t_learn_in_school_42643.html.

Kaliszewski, Michael. 2020. "Substance Abuse Statistics for African Americans." American Addiction Centers. July 29, 2020. https://americanaddictioncenters.org/rehab-guide/addiction-statistics/african-americans.

Margo, Robert A. 1994. *Race and Schooling in the South, 1880-1950: An Economic History*. Chicago: University Of Chicago Press.

Mohatt NV, Thompson AB, Thai ND, Tebes JK. "Historical trauma as public narrative: a conceptual review of how history impacts present-day health." Social Science & Medicine (1982). 2014 Apr; 106:128-136. DOI: 10.1016/j.socscimed.2014.01.043. PMID: 24561774; PMCID: PMC4001826.

Office of Minority Mental Health, US Department of Health and Human Services (2016). Mental health and African Americans. Accessed March 15, 2022. http://minorityhealth.hhs.gov/omh/browse.aspx?lvl=4&lvlid=24)

Straussner, Shulamith, Ashenberg, Lala, Calnan, Alexandrea Josephine. "Trauma Through the Life Cycle: A Review of Current Literature." In: Clinical Social Work Journal. 2014; Vol. 42, No. 4. pp. 323-335.

Vora, MD, Ellen. "Can Trauma Really Be 'Stored' in the Body?" December 11, 2019. https://ellenvora.com/can-trauma-really-be-stored-in-the-body/.

www.ingramcontent.com/pod-product-compliance
Lightning Source LLC
Chambersburg PA
CBHW020918160726
47993CB00005B/2034